THE RAPTURE OF POLITICS

THE RAPTURE OF POLITICS

The
Christian
Right as the
United States
Approaches the
year 2000

edited by
**Steve Bruce, Peter Kivisto
and William H. Swatos, Jr.**

with an introduction by Peter Kivisto

Transaction Publishers
New Brunswick (U.S.A.) and London (U.K.)

Library of Congress Catalog Number: 94-28321
ISBN: 1-56000-802-4
Printed in the United States of America

Library of Congress Cataloging-in-Publication Data

The rapture of politics: the Christian right as the United States approaches the year 2000/edited by Steve Bruce, Peter Kivisto, and William H. Swatos, Jr. with an introduction by Peter Kivisto.
  "Simultaneously published as volume 55, number 3 of Sociology of religion: a quarterly review"—Pref.
  Includes bibliographical references and index.
  ISBN 1-56000-802-4

  1. Evangelicalism—United States—History—20th century. 2. Fundamentalism—History. 3. Christianity and politics—Protestant churches—History—20th century. 4. Conservatism—Religious aspects—Christianity—History of doctrines—20th century. 5. Conservatism—United States—History—20th century. 6. United States—Politics and government—1945-1989. 7. United States—Politics and government—1989-1993. 8. United States—Politics and government—1993- 9. United States—Church history—20th century. I. Bruce, Steve, 1954- . II. Kivisto, Peter, 1948- . III. Swatos, William H.
BR1642.U5R37 1994
320.5'5'097309049—dc20   94-28321
                                                                        CIP

IN MEMORIAM

JOSEPH H. FICHTER

Contents

[T]he early Christians knew full well the world is governed by demons and that he who lets himself in for politics, that is, for power and force as means, contracts with diabolical powers and for his action it is *not* true that good can follow only from good and evil only from evil, but that often the opposite is true. Anyone who fails to see this is, indeed, a political infant.

Max Weber
Politik als Beruf, 1919

Preface

This volume is being simultaneously co-published as volume 55, number 3 of *Sociology of Religion: A Quarterly Review* and in book form by Transaction Publishers. I am grateful to Irving Louis Horowitz, Scott Bramson, and Mary E. Curtis of Transaction, and to Karen Simkanin of A & A Printing for the spirit of cooperation that they manifested to bring this collection to the reader in timely fashion. *Sociology of Religion* is wholly owned and independently published by the Association for the Sociology of Religion.

I am also grateful to Steve Bruce whose suggestion in November of 1992 that we undertake this collection came like a soft breeze of Indian summer before hard Illinois winter. He recruited the articles. Peter Kivisto was responsible for vetting the submissions, eliciting substantive revisions, and recommending the final selections and their arrangement. He also kindly agreed to write the introduction at a busy time in my life. The collection did not come without striving. Some potential contributors whose work we desired were unable or unwilling to provide something. In another case, we came to the conclusion that a piece we solicited envisioned a different kind of book from what we intended, and we seemed simply unable to achieve a level of reciprocal understanding necessary for acceptance. I assume responsibility for the final editing, and for the epilogue, which is not part of the journal version and which may make everything that seems relatively clear in the substantive chapters a little muddier. This reflects my conviction, with Max Weber, that though humans are "rational actors," there are multiple and competing *rationales* constantly in contention within our minds and bodies, and among our social and economic relations.

This volume is dedicated to the memory of an outstanding sociologist of religion, a friend and colleague who was never afraid to confront the interpenetrating dynamics of religion and politics. A portion of the income from the sales of this book will support the Fichter Fund of the Association for the Sociology of Religion, currently designated to assist research on women and religion.

WHS, Jr.
Cambridge, Illinois

Introduction

The Rise or Fall of the Christian Right? Conflicting Reports from the Frontline

Peter Kivisto
Augustana College-Illinois

Perhaps because I first read these essays while teaching in London in the fall of 1993, I thought more intently about the issue of the distinctiveness of the religious Right in America than I otherwise would have. It was clearly on my mind when I attended services at the Countess of Huntingdon Connexion chapel in St. Ives, Cornwall. In a cold, damp building that was in great need of repair, the twenty or so parishioners — mainly pensioners — were entreated by the pastor to write letters to their local MP protesting pending parliamentary legislation that would abolish Sunday closing laws. Not an issue of great importance to the American religious Right, but at least here was evidence of a theologically conservative religious body seeking to influence the political system.

However, I came away convinced, not that there is a parallel to be drawn, but that there is something unique about the American scene. It was less the issue than the approach or tone that suggested that what I was observing was different from the political involvements of the American Christian Right. At bedrock, what was lacking in St. Ives was a level of intensity that would have suggested that the members of the congregation genuinely viewed themselves as a vanguard of societal transformation. Rather there was a ritualistic (in a Mertonian, not a liturgical, sense) quality to this call to action in the midst of the service. It appeared to this outsider that the minister and the parishioners acutely sensed the limits of their capacity to influence the course of this legislation.

But do members of the Christian Right in America actually see themselves as a vanguard? They certainly do, according to journalist Christopher Reed. In the 2 November 1993 issue of the British daily newspaper, *The Guardian*, he writes with fear and loathing of the "insidious rise of the religious right," describing the movement's activist core as "not just religious crusaders, but revolutionaries" (pp. 2-3). The issue at hand that prompted the article was the then pending referendum in California, Proposition 174, which would have provided educational vouchers to students attending private and religious schools. Reed observed that the chances of passage were slim, a reflection of the larger situation for the Christian Right, namely that it is in a period of retrenchment. Nonetheless, he concluded with a message: it is necessary to be on the alert since "the religious right in America remains, militant and busy."

If Reed is correct, this is a cause for alarm for critics, and a reason for jubilation for religious Right adherents. But in spite of their militancy and their activism, how significant a factor are they in the current political climate in America? Is the Christian Right a spent social movement, or has it become a durable feature of the political landscape as we approach the *fin de siècle*? Is it and will it in the foreseeable future exist on the margins, or is it and will it be a viable force in defining the core values of the American polity?

The chapters contained herein provide varied provisional answers to these and related questions. This book is devoted to assessing the current impact of the New Christian Right (NCR) on American politics. It, thus, constitutes a stocktaking of the NCR in the early 1990s. When Steve Bruce approached Bill Swatos about the possibility of a special issue, Bruce was — as his opening chapter clearly indicates — convinced that now that the dust had settled, we were in a position to assess somewhat more dispassionately the role of the NCR in the political battles and culture wars that have been waged in the United States since at least the 1970s. Moreover, he was convinced that the evidence will lead us to see not only that the strength of the NCR during its heyday has been overestimated by many observers, but also that factors which led to its "inevitable failure" were not seen or were not treated with sufficient seriousness.

The contributors to this issue were selected by Steve Bruce with the objective of providing readers with a provocative forum. Thus, there was no effort to assemble a group of sociologists who agreed with his own assessments. Far from it. Since Bruce's critical sights are aimed at Jeffrey Hadden, he invited Hadden to contribute an article. Hadden, unfortunately, declined. But those with conclusions similar to Hadden's — most notably perhaps John Simpson, James M. Penning, and Matthew C. Moen — are represented here, along with scholars who fall somewhere in between the two positions. Moreover, it is not too difficult to detect in some pieces a certain disdain for the NCR, while in at least two there is evidence of genuine sympathy for the movement. In short, this is, if not exactly ecumenical, at the very least a decidedly diverse assemblage.

To make their respective cases, the contributors have had to come to terms with the knotty question about what does and what does not fall under the umbrella of the NCR. Aside from the agreed upon assumption that the NCR involves theologically conservative Protestants who have entered the political arena with an agenda that is at once political and religious, there is little evidence of consensus about who falls within and who without the NCR fold. If seen as a subset of conservative Protestants, as Stephen D. Johnson suggests is the case, what differentiates the NCR from the non-NCR component? Neither he nor the other contributors provide an answer, or at least an entirely satisfactory answer, to the question. Without the benefit of particular definitions proffered by various contributors, one senses that such terms as evangelical, fundamentalist, and conservative Protestant are frequently being used in somewhat different ways.

Definitions count. Those who operate with the most stringent definitions of the NCR, not surprisingly, tend to treat it as a more limited phenomenon with considerably less possibility of impacting the polity over the long term in a sustained and profound way. On the other hand, the sociological latitudinarians are capable of seeing America on the verge of a dramatically new political reconfiguration. This, it is argued, can be seen in the growing polarization among the electorate over moral issues. It can also be seen in the NCR's institutionalization in the political process and in its success in redefining the central cultural values of the Republican party.

If treated as a social movement, relying on a core of dedicated and energetic true believers, the NCR is correctly depicted as attracting a distinct minority of the United States population. However, if seen as a voting bloc, and measured in terms of support for a variety of social issues such as abortion and prayer in schools, the NCR would appear to elicit considerably more support — though just how much is a matter of considerable debate. Moreover, if viewed as a social movement, it is possible to draw differing conclusions depending on the implicit or explicit understanding of social movements. If seen in cyclic terms, it is possible to conclude that the NCR will run its course in the near future, much like the fate of the New Left by the mid-1970s. However, with a somewhat different orientation regarding social movements (perhaps inspired by resource mobilization theory), it is possible to see a movement transforming itself into a more or less durable institutional presence capable of dealing with the politics of everyday life.

Writing from the same side of the Atlantic as Christopher Reed, Steve Bruce draws markedly different conclusions about the future viability of the NCR than his journalist fellow citizen. Bruce takes aim at sociologists of religion who, in his estimation, have exaggerated the strength of the NCR. He uses the NCRs general lack of success in achieving their legislative and judicial goals (only limited success on the defensive agenda and persistent frustration with its offensive agenda) as a general indicator of the "inevitable failure" of the NCR.

Bruce also briefly addresses a topic that is the central focus of several pieces: electoral politics. Articles by Clyde Wilcox; Stephen Johnson; Phillip Hammond, Mark A. Shibley, and Peter M. Solow; James M. Penning; and Lyman A. Kellstedt, John C. Green, James L. Guth, and Corwin E. Smidt take up in various ways the matter of the electoral involvements of the NCR during the 1980s and early 1990s.

Wilcox, like Bruce, sees the NCR as capable of attracting only a limited electoral following. While it is possible to win elections at the local level, both think that similar success becomes increasingly difficult at the state and national levels, where coalition building and centrist politics become increasingly necessary in order to be successful at the polls.

Johnson's contribution reports on factors related to voting patterns of Catholics, mainline Protestants, and conservative Protestants in Muncie, Indiana. Not surprisingly, he found that conservative social issues played a role in determining the voting preferences of conservative Protestants. Their voting choices were less determined by economic issues than by cultural ones. However, as Johnson sees things, the NCR lies within conservative Protestantism as a subset that takes "extreme positions" that are not shared by fellow conservatives and will not permit a broader base of political support. In other words, far more people agree with vague notions about the need to strengthen families and to promote social responsibility, than with NCR positions on issues such as abortion and prayer in public schools. Johnson suggests that a broader, more tolerant conservative Protestantism has the potential for being a significant political force for some time to come, while the NCR's efforts will likely end in frustration. His assessment, in fundamental respects, dovetails with the predictions of both Bruce and Wilcox.

Phillip Hammond and his colleagues observe that the main fault line between conservatives and liberals is no longer chiefly a debate over theological issues. Nor, due to the end of the Cold War, can anticommunism play the role it once did. Thus, at the present we are left with a battle over the issue of "family values." John Simpson sees a similar divide in the politics of the 1980s, but rather than describing this as a battle over family values, he locates this in terms of — and without ever referring to Foucault — the politics of the body. In particular, Simpson singles out the debates over abortion and homosexuality as signifying the most potent cultural divisions by the late 1980s.

Hammond *et al.* do not appear to think that the NCR has managed to capture the ideological core of the Republican party. But they remain unconvinced that Richard Nixon was correct in believing that the party should dump, in Nixon's words, the "religious fanatics" lest they alienate its traditional bases of support as well as potential crossover voters. Simpson reminds readers of the fluidity of current trends and cautions that his findings must be provisional.

In contrast, Lyman A. Kellstedt and colleagues treat the 1992 presidential election as potentially a watershed event, marking the beginning of a new set of political alliances and a dramatic new cleavage in the two-party system. Billing the election as both the "Year of the Evangelical" and the "Year of the Secular," they claim that seculars have moved ever more firmly into the Democratic party, and now can be seen as defining that party's cultural core. At the same time, the disaffection of many mainline Protestants from the Republican party has occurred simultaneously with the binding of evangelicals to that party in a manner that puts them now in a position to define the party's cultural core. In this account, the precise role of mainline Protestants remains rather nebulous. That they might play a mediating role or operate as power brokers moving strategically from one camp to the other as the issue and the situation dictates is never considered. Instead, the overarching impression one gets from this piece — more so than from the Hammond *et al.* contribution — is that polarization in the "culture wars" is likely to increase in the future.

James M. Penning and Matthew C. Moen address, in a more sustained way than the other essays, issues related to NCR organizations and their place in the political arena at the moment and in the foreseeable future. Both present accounts that, with differing nuances and emphases, suggest the NCR remains a force to be reckoned with. Their prognostications are made with an awareness of considerable retrenchment since the early 1980s. Indeed, Moen provides a table reporting the dissolution of groups such as the Moral Majority, Freedom Council, National Christian Action Coalition, and American Coalition for Traditional Values and the moribund status of others, including the Religious Roundtable and the Christian Voice. Whereas Wilcox discusses some of the institutional impediments that jeopardized the efficacy of the Moral Majority and views its demise in terms of social movement cycles, Penning and Moen see the present as a period of retooling and readjusting.

Penning uses the Pat Robertson campaign as a case study of the struggle for control of the Republican party between party professionals loyal to George Bush and NCR amateurs. Despite the serious divisions that have been inflicted on the GOP, he sees the NCR as a potential source of revitalization of the party. This is possible, he contends, insofar as the NCR adopts a more tolerant approach. In other words, coexistence is possible between the NCR and the traditional backbone of the Republican party, which includes many who embrace a libertarian strain of political conservatism that is not enthusiastic about government involvement in people's private lives. Unlike Kellstedt and colleagues, Penning does not suggest that the NCR has captured the soul of the Republican party. Rather, he looks to the possibility of the two camps accommodating to each other in a fashion that will insure that the party does not move too far from the political center, where it would be rendered ineffectual in national elections. The evidence for an increasingly tolerant and pragmatic stance on the part of the NCR is rather anecdotal and not especially convincing. The question that Penning fails to address is the cost of moderation to the mobilization of activism.

Moen's article traces the same history as Penning, albeit from a more panoramic vantage. Moen periodizes the movement into the expansionist, transition, and institutionalization phases. Like Penning, he sees the NCR as adapting more conventional political forms, but he does not speak to the matter of whether or not the content has also changed. If the transition period constitutes something of a nadir for the movement, Moen suggests that since 1987 movement leaders have learned from past mistakes and have adjusted appropriately. He sees the use of "rights" language and campaigns at the grassroots, such as local school board elections, as indicators of a readjustment that will broaden the appeal of the NCR without necessarily jeopardizing its ability to mobilize its activist core.

Like Bruce and Wilcox, I am not convinced. It is not clear to me that the attempt to employ rights language will succeed. Far from accepting this use of rights language, some sectors of the public may see it as an attempt to coopt or distort what they perceive to be a proper use of rights language. Part of the problem the NCR has is in convincing outsiders that it is a victimized minority whose rights have been violated. Not only opponents, but also many who are either vaguely sympathetic or neutral toward the NCR in general, have a hard time seeing the NCR as downtrodden and oppressed. More significantly, I think it is far easier to make a case that the recourse to stealth candidates constitutes weakness than, as Moen would appear to suggest, that it is an indication of political maturation.

What is clear is that the NCR has not disappeared and is not likely to do so. It will remain a part of the religious and political landscape. But this new essay collection of significant substantive scholarship provides ample testimony to the claim that social scientists are far from consensus over the matter of where the NCR will be located in that landscape — on the fringes or in the center, in the forefront or in the background — and thus argues for its continued salience to assessments of political and religious life in the United States.

1

The Inevitable Failure of
the New Christian Right

Steve Bruce
University of Aberdeen

This chapter attempts to gauge the impact of the New Christian Right (NCR), to draw attention to features of the movement and its environment that limit its effectiveness, and finally to offer a tentative explanation of the exaggerated responses to the movement. I suggest that there is an elective affinity between over-estimating the NCR and misunderstanding that body of ideas and propositions known (usually to its critics) as "secularization theory."

MEASURING IMPACT

It is no easy thing to estimate the influence of a major social movement. First, it is difficult to specify just what would count as "turning America around" and "bringing God back into public life." To mention an example discussed shortly, is it an NCR victory if the Supreme Court on entirely secular grounds makes a judgment on abortion that is unpopular with the "pro-choice" lobby? Second, as is often the case with what Blumer (1978) called general social movements, it is not always clear which individuals and organizations constitute the new Christian or religious Right. Some groups involved in trying to influence school management deny NCR links yet are accused by anti-NCR organizations of being "stealth" candidates (Kelly 1993:2). Third, impact of an extremely abstract and long-term nature may be claimed (for example, "an increasingly conservative moral climate") which, even if the change can be established, offers little or no chance of demonstrating causal connections. Fourth, we may overlook the possibly biasing interests of certain sources of information. People For the American Way (PFAW), the most prominent anti-NCR campaigning organization, has an obvious interest in making the wolf at the door seem as fierce as possible, but its glosses on public events are often taken up by others and reported as neutral accounts. The PFAW report on NCR activities in the 1992 elections seems to have echoes across a wide range of media.

Nonetheless, with all these reservations, some sort of evaluation must be attempted. So as to minimize duplication with other chapters in this book, I will concentrate on legislative and judicial change and, one of the preconditions for movement in those areas, electoral power.

THE NCR AND THE LAW

John Garvey has recently summarized the New Christian Right's judicial and legislative record under the headings of "defensive" and "offensive" agenda. The movement has achieved most with what are clearly religious claims in the private sphere (for example, trying to protect religious schools from state regulation), and it has usually succeeded by following failures in court with legislative action to give specific protection. Thus in 1979, after a state court upheld a scheme for regulating private schools, the North Carolina state legislature passed a law enacting that "in matters of education . . . No human authority shall, in any case whatever, control or interfere with the rights of conscience" (1993:40), a view that many people outside the NCR could equally readily endorse. What Garvey calls the fundamentalist "defensive agenda" has also had some success in claiming rights such as access to public facilities for private activity. In 1990, the Supreme Court upheld the federal Equal Access Act against objections that it was unconstitutional in bringing religion into the public sphere. A Moral Majority officer commenting on that case said:

> For the first three years of our existence we framed the issues wrong. We pushed for school prayer but we framed the issue in terms of how prayer in schools is good. But some people feel that prayer in school is bad. So we learned to frame the issue in terms of "students rights." . . . We are pro-choice for students having the right to pray in public schools (in Hertzke 1990:70).

However, it has only successfully deployed appeals to fairness on a very narrow ground. Its attempts to use fairness as a principle for requiring schools to balance the teaching of evolutionary accounts of the origins of species with equal time for "creation science" alternatives have failed. With by all accounts very little thought for the consequences, for example, the Arkansas legislature passed an equal time bill. The American Civil Liberties Union (ACLU) took the bill to the courts in 1981 to argue that it was an unconstitutional requirement to support a particular religion. The creationists had to persuade the judge that someone who did not accept the authority of the Bible would nonetheless find their account as compatible with the evidence and with scientific method as that of the evolutionists. They failed miserably to present a case that was consistent, let alone plausible. The bill was struck down (Gilkey 1985). A very similar bill from the Louisiana legislature was taken to the Supreme Court where, by the very considerable margin of 7 to 2, it was judged unconstitutional: "[t]he purpose of the Creationism Act was to restructure the science curriculum to conform with a particular religious viewpoint . . . [and] because the primary purpose of the Creationism Act is to endorse a particular religious doctrine, the Act furthers religion in violation of the Establishment Clause (Supreme Court of the United States, 85-1513, 19 June 1987:13-14).

The fairness principle was also employed to argue that "secular humanism" (a supposedly coherent package of beliefs which are united mainly by their lack of support for traditional Christian propositions) was a religion and that evenhandedness required that, if Christian values and perspectives were to be banned from schools, so too should the secular humanist alternatives. With assistance from Pat Robertson's National Legal Foundation, over 600 fundamentalists filed suit against the Alabama State Board of Education, charging that the Board had violated their constitutional rights. Judge W. Brevard Hand found for the plaintiffs, but the unanimous verdict of the three Appeals Court judges was that he was wrong in accepting that all knowledge could come in only two forms so that anything which was not patently Christian must be secular humanist. The Appeals Court applied the narrower test of whether the text books at issue taught an identifiable philosophy of secular humanism and concluded that they did not. As with the creation science cases, the fundamentalists had some initial success in presenting themselves as a disadvantaged minority but lost the argument as soon as the apparent symmetry between theism and humanism was scrutinized in detail.

Finally, it is worth noting a Tennessee judgment with profound implications for the limits of the fairness argument. In overturning the judgment of a lower court, the Sixth Circuit Appeals Court unanimously stated that requiring children to read books that did not endorse their beliefs or even which challenged their beliefs was not an infringement of their constitutional rights. They ruled that the earlier decision had failed to distinguish between simply reading or talking about other beliefs and being compelled or persuaded to adopt them.

The NCR has had little success on what Garvey calls its "offensive agenda": the use of law to regulate people's behavior. In 1986 the Supreme Court held that the Due Process clause did not protect homosexual sodomy. However, in so doing the Court was explicitly returning the issue to the elected branches of government to deal with "and there the tide is running against the fundamentalist side. States are with increasing frequency repealing or refusing to enforce their laws against sodomy" (1993:41). The same is the case with abortion. The Court has recently made three significant decisions. It has expressed unhappiness about the trimester rules laid down by Roe. It has allowed the government to restrict public funding for abortions. And it has permitted states to require (with some exceptions) that minors notify their parents before having abortions. But once again these restrictions have been upheld for nonreligious reasons, and the Court has not outlawed abortion. It has simply handed the issue back to the legislatures, where the fundamentalist record is at best mixed. Louisiana and Utah have enacted restrictive time laws. Iowa, Minnesota and New York have restricted public funds for abortions. Arizona, Arkansas, Michigan, Mississippi, North Dakota, Nebraska, South Carolina, and Tennessee have enacted laws designed to ensure parental consent or notice for minors, or informed consent for adults. On the other side of the balance, attempts to restrict abortions have failed in Alabama, Florida, Idaho, Illinois, and South Dakota. And Maryland and Connecticut have passed laws designed to preserve the right to abortion in the event of Roe v. Wade being overturned. Furthermore, the interest of Hillary Clinton will ensure that federal administrative action does not curtail access to abortions.

Finally, a major part of the offensive agenda was concerned with competition over what, after the model of Weber's "ethnic honor" (1968:391), we might term "religious honor": the assertion of "the excellence of one's own customs and the inferiority of alien ones." The NCR wanted public support for acts of religious worship and for the symbols of its distinctive religious culture. Despite the appointment by Reagan and Bush of five "conservative" justices, the Supreme Court has followed the precedents of the earlier courts in refusing to permit government support for such acts and symbols.

This rather poor showing for the NCR has to be seen in the context of eight years of a Reagan presidency and four years of Bush. That Clinton now has four years to make his own court appointments (and has already committed himself to a pro-choice position on abortion and to the promotion of homosexual rights) suggests that this is the best they will do.

POLITICS

As Garvey notes, the main point of the small changes in the position of the courts on NCR issues has been to return them to the legislative arm of government. Indeed the fact that the Supreme Court in 1992 heard only half the number of cases heard a decade ago (and most of them were matters of statutory interpretation with little political impact) suggests a general shift in public policy making back from the courts to the elected legislatures. Rather curiously, this is often seen by liberals as a victory for the Right. It would only be such if, as Falwell and other NCR leaders argue, it were the case that the courts have been used to impose unpopular liberal positions. What it more accurately means is that sociomoral issues will increasingly be determined in the democratic political arena of elections and referenda. Hence in evaluating the NCR we should now turn to electoral politics.

Judging NCR success in this area is no easy matter. Proponents of competing evaluations can readily list any number of election contests from 1980 to the present to show either that NCR support helped win or helped lose seats. Some commentators blame Bush's 1992 defeat on the religious right hijacking the Republican party platform. Others argue that he lost because he showed insufficient commitment to that platform (for example, by allowing his wife and the wife of the vice-president informally to offer journalists less radical views on abortion than those enshrined in the platform). Spokesmen for the American Coalition for Traditional Values believe that Roger Jepsen of Iowa lost his senate seat in 1984 to a Mondale Democrat because he turned his back on the religious right which had supposedly helped him win in 1978 (McLaughlin 1984). It was widely held by commentators that Virginia got its first black governor in 1990 because his white opponent was vocally pro-life until he discovered it was costing him the election (Brogan 1991). Western Massachusetts now has a Democratic Congressman for the first time in its history because he was pro-choice and his Republican opponent was pro-life.

One way of abbreviating the process of argument by trading cases is to note that one can find hardly anyone since 1980 claiming major electoral victories for the NCR. Not even NCR spokesmen or conservative sympathizers have often made such claims, which come most frequently from anti-NCR organizations such as People For the American Way, whose obvious interest has already been mentioned. Where NCR organizations and their critics appear to agree is that the NCR has shifted its attention from important large constituency elections

(Congressional or gubernatorial, for example) to small constituency elections that are severally unimportant (school boards, for example). In 1989 a reporter for the *Wall Street Journal* quoted NCR activists saying "The Falwell-Robertson phenomenon was the first wave. The second wave is forming. It's grass roots activism. It's not co-ordinated; it's not national" (Schribman 1989). This shift is itself good evidence that the NCR has failed to make much impact in the major league. There is also agreement that efforts are now being directed to "infiltrating" the Republican party by turning NCR activists into Republican party activists. To the extent that this trend continues and endures, it is likely to produce at best a Pyrrhic victory. Like the militant Left's influence on the British Labour Party in the early 1980s, the NCR's effect on the Republican party will be to shift it away from the middle ground which it needs to occupy if it is to win major elections.

None of what I have said is intended to deny the very obvious point that in small units where conservatives are numerous, the NCR can achieve legislative and electoral success. As I have repeatedly argued, in contrast to the much more monolithic structures of the old world, the federal structure of the United States permits locales a considerable degree of freedom (Bruce 1988). However, as one moves up from the city and county to the congressional district and the state to the federal government, one moves to units of greater cultural, social and political diversity, and one sees the potential for such pressure groups as the NCR steadily diminished. Furthermore, the centripetal structure of the courts and the fact that many NCR issues concern fundamental rights means that the final judgment will often lie with the cosmopolitan center and not with the locale. Judge Brevard Hand's district of Alabama might be sympathetic to fundamentalist criticism of secular humanism, but his views will always be subordinate to those of either the Supreme Court or, insofar as the Court returns such issues to the legislative branch of government, to a larger electorate.

SUBTLE EFFECTS

In later reflecting on their *Prime-Time Preachers*, Hadden and Swann wrote "our intent was to argue that, notwithstanding the limited impact of the New Christian Right on the 1980 elections, their potential as a significant political force should not be measured in terms of that election, or even the 1982 and 1984 elections, for that matter" (1982:9). One might interpret this as suggesting that claims for NCR influence were outside the scope of empirical social science, but to be more charitable one can agree that the fact that the NCR has failed to make much progress as an electoral force or won any major victories in the courts does not of itself mean that it has been entirely without consequence. One may argue, as Falwell and others have frequently done, that the NCR has had a considerable success in reestablishing the respectability of conservative sociomoral positions and in reasserting the right of fundamentalists to be taken seriously. It is certainly the case that the last decade has seen considerable publicity given to NCR activists and their views. The presidential campaign of Pat Robertson, though pointless as an exercise in electoral politics, brought the NCR unprecedented exposure. However, while such publicity ensures a public debate, it only guarantees to win that debate if it is the case that the previously dominant values and attitudes represented liberal hegemony rather than popular preference.

The NCR has also seen (a) the "mobilization" of fundamentalists (particularly in voter registration for a constituency that previously had a poor record of voting), and (b) the training of a cadre of fundamentalists in the techniques of pressure group politics. Both of these will be of considerable benefit to the NCR in leveling the playing field of American sociomoral contests, but their impact must be judged in the context of opponents of the NCR doing the same or more.

To conclude this very brief review, the NCR began with a great many advantages. It has enjoyed considerable access to the mass media through the products of televangelists such as Falwell and Robertson. It was able to use the direct mailing techniques and mailing lists of televangelism organizations to reach its potential supporters economically. It was led by some extremely skilled (self) publicists. It was able to make use of the excellent existing networks of conservative Protestant pastors. Nonetheless, the considered judgment of most uncommitted observers is that the movement has failed to achieve significant progress on items that were specific to its agenda (as distinct from those ambitions, such as increased defense spending, that were shared with mainstream conservatives). Ed Mate, a former political director of the Republican National Committee concluded: "The evangelicals' impact on Washington politics has been minimal. The things they have been disappointed with have greatly outnumbered the things they have been pleased with" (in Aikman 1988:23).

SOCIAL FUNCTIONS AND MOVEMENT FRACTIONS

I would like now to explain the failure of the NCR. Or to put it another way, I want to draw attention to features of the NCR and its environment that, had they been properly attended to in, say, 1980, would have led to a realistic assessment of the movement.

First, there is a very obvious point that was widely overlooked in the first few years of responding to the Moral Majority, and that is the lack of consensus among conservative Protestants. All too often some ball-park figure for the membership of all conservative Protestant denominations, or the "pray TV" audience, or Americans claiming a born again experience was posited as the potential recruitment base for the NCR. As Smidt (1989) and Wilcox (1986) pointed out (and note the rather late date at which the point started to be made), there were major differences among fundamentalists, evangelicals and pentecostalists, not only about religious beliefs and sociomoral issues but also about the appropriateness of various sorts of campaigning on those things about which they did agree.

Second, quite inappropriate comparisons were made between the NCR and religiopolitical movements elsewhere, often in countries with quite different economic and political structures. The grouping of the NCR with Iranian extremism and Protestant Unionism in Ulster, as Hadden and Shupe (1986) do in the introduction to a collection on *Prophetic Religions* and as Marty and Appleby (1991, 1993) do in their "Fundamentalism Project," confuses rather than illuminates. First, the more one stresses continuities between Islamic movements and the NCR, the more one loses sight of the fact that social structure is a consideration in individual action. The United States is a culturally pluralistic affluent industrial democracy with a complex and stable civic society. Egypt and Iran are not.

But even if one takes the more apposite comparison of the NCR and Ulster or Afrikaner conservative Protestant politics, it still misses the point that there is all the difference in the world between the part played by religion in the politics of ethnic conflict and state formation, and in the politics of pressure groups competing with a stable democratic nation-state. It simplifies, of course, but we can think of the difference in terms of the classic distinction between ascribed and achieved identity. Ulster Protestants have a history of religio-ethnic conflict with Irish Catholics as long as their sojourn in Ireland (more than 300 years). To be born a Protestant is to be placed in one camp on an historic battlefield. That the fundamental issue of the border and sovereignty has not been resolved means that religious and ethnic identity remain firmly wedded. One can abandon one only by abandoning the other and at considerable social cost; people are killed for rejecting their ascribed identity. The conflicts that motivate involvement in the NCR are much less pressing on the participants, are a product of individual choice, and can be altered at little personal cost.

Although there is not space to pursue the point here, it is also worth noting a theological difference between American fundamentalists and Ulster (and Afrikaner) Protestants (see Bruce 1986; Wallis and Bruce 1986). The former tend to be Arminian; the latter tend to be Calvinist. This apparently small theological point has important implications for individualism which, I have argued, partly explain why Ulster and Afrikaner Protestants have a very long and consistent history of religio-ethnic politics, while the political involvements of American fundamentalists tend to be cyclical.

Third, what was abundantly clear to the leaders of the NCR (and to such vociferous opponents within fundamentalism as Bob Jones III) was that the "moral majority" was not a majority and could achieve its goals only through alliances with other groups: conservative blacks, Catholics and Jews. This in turn required a flexibility, a willingness to cut deals and overlook aspects of the beliefs of one's allies, which is quite at odds with the key premise of most varieties of conservative Protestantism, which identify themselves precisely by contrasting their supposed consistency across all spheres of life with the liberal Protestant acceptance of a division between the public and the private. The NCR required its supporters to alternate between religious thinking (in which only born-again Bible-believing fundamentalists are saved) and political thinking (in which one seeks to mobilize around a shared Judeo-Christian heritage or, even more broadly, around conservative values). While leaders such as Falwell managed to alternate, many of the foot soldiers could not. There was thus always a paradox at the heart of the NCR. The reason for getting involved in politics was the belief that the confinement of religiously derived values to the private world and to voluntary associations was an offense to God. The mark of the true Christian is the desire to reestablish God's righteous kingdom or earth and to protest against error. Yet in order to pursue that agenda effectively, the true Christian had periodically to overlook the heresies of Romanism, Judaism, and every other form of conservative Protestantism.

Two problems result from this. The first is that many fundamentalists could not sustain their political involvement for long. In 1984 and again in 1986, I interviewed many fundamentalists in Virginia and South Carolina and found in their conversation recurring statements of disillusionment with the compromises of the political process in which they had become involved in 1979 or 1980. I would not claim this explains the following data, but it is worth noting that, despite voter registration drives, in 1984 fundamentalists (36.5 percent) were more likely than evangelicals (33.9) and nonevangelicals (25.5) to have abstained (Jelen 1987).

The second problem of alliances is that many potential allies remained profoundly suspicious of the NCR. Catholics could easily remember that the people who now solicited their assistance in anti-abortion crusades were the same people who previously campaigned against them. Tamney and Johnson's work shows Middletown Catholics no keener on religious involvement in politics than liberal Protestants (1987). That Catholics had good reasons to be suspicious can be seen from one of Wilcox's articles about the Ohio Moral Majority chapter (1987b) which, he notes, preceded a meeting to discuss alliances with nonfundamentalists groups with a talk on "The Roman Catholic Church: Harlot of Rome"! Kellstedt (1989) notes that anti-Catholicism was a significant predictor of Moral Majority support among evangelicals. The alliance between the Archdiocese of New York and Pat Robertson's Christian Coalition to put out voter guides for the 1993 New York school board elections is an interesting departure, for it is the first time that the Catholic Church has been involved in a recent NCR campaign. What the consequences will be is not yet clear, but two points are worth noting. First, as it usually tries to do, the Church has set the agenda for its members. Second, it has become involved in a city where it is in a strong position and thus has little reason to fear that an NCR campaign will become an anti-Catholic campaign. The first point reminds us of the institutional strength of the Catholic Church and suggests a model of operation which, because it offends against the individualistic conscience assumed by democratic politics in a pluralistic culture, is unlikely to be popular, even with many of its own members. The second point suggests geographical constraints on Protestant-Catholic alliances.

There have been enough instances of fundamentalist NCR leaders making off-hand anti-Semitic remarks to give Jews cause for concern. In a back-handed introduction to a pro-Zionist speech, Falwell told his audience: "A few of you here don't like Jews. And I know why. He [sic] can make more money accidentally than you can on purpose" (Conway and Siegelman 1982:168). The reluctance of black conservative Protestants to become involved (even if they overlooked the liberal economic and antistatist agenda of the NCR) can be readily understood if one considers that, public rhetoric notwithstanding, one of the purposes of the independent Christian schools attached to many white fundamentalist churches is to maintain racial segregation.

Much of the social science research on the NCR consists of attitude surveys. What is well known but sometimes forgotten is that there are many considerations that intervene between an opinion, an attitude, a belief or a value, and action predicated on such mental states. Insufficient attention has been given to the need for opportunities to act and the relative costs of different courses of action. To return to an observation made above, whether the internal tensions within any movement will subvert it is often a matter of opportunity. In the 1930s two anti-Catholic political parties, respectively the Scottish Protestant League and Protestant Action, won seats in the local councils of Glasgow and Edinburgh. The five and seven members elected soon found that except on issues that had a clear sectarian dimension, they voted against each other. Their single issue was all that united them, and they were unable to dominate the council business agenda sufficiently to keep sectarian issues uppermost. Hence more often than not they voted against each other, and not surprisingly, their parties collapsed (Bruce 1985). American fundamentalists, pentecostalists and evangelicals are not much of a religious suchness nor are they socioeconomically homogenous. The call to think as members of the Moral Majority is a call that competes with the other sources of identity and action, and the extent to which it takes precedence is largely determined by a public agenda over which the NCR has little control. Bill "Slick Willie" Clinton became president because more people were concerned about the weakness of George Bush's economic policy than were concerned about Clinton's support for promoting the rights of women and homosexuals.

There is a paradox at the heart of movements that seek to elevate single-issues pressure-group politics into broad party campaigns. Sustaining the involvement of pressure groups against the divergent interests of their supporters on issues other than those that are the focus of pressure group work requires activists to stress their issue, but this backfires in democratic politics because the stress on the common themes that unite the supporters alienates nonsupporters (who suppose that the candidate or the activists have nothing to offer on other matters). Indeed, it seems clear that single-issue candidates alienate even those who support their stand on the single issue. Any number of polls during Robertson's election campaign showed that even many of those who shared his sociomoral positions and his religion were less, rather than more, likely to vote for him because he was a televangelist and an ordained cleric. Johnson et al. (1990:300) have an illuminating observation from a defeated Christian Right congressional candidate:

> Lynch said he suffered from the dilemma facing all Christian right candidates. Such candidates begin their campaigns emphasising moral issues because that gets them volunteers and financial support. But, the media tags Christian right candidates as moral issue candidates and plays up their positions on such issues; for instance, interviewers spend all their time on moral issues. The result is that Christian right candidates cannot get across their secular message.

This suggests (a) that the NCR will do better in referenda which bind legislators rather than in electoral contests, and (b) that they will do better if they support established Republican conservatives who are Right on some of the moral issues than if they promote their own moral issues candidates.

One further caution about the NCR's influence that should have been entered in 1980 but was sadly often over-looked was that the NCR had powerful opponents. Successful NCR mobilizations alerted and aroused those who were opposed to such involvement (including those who sympathized with the positions taken but thought that it is procedurally wrong for Christians to do Christian politics). The conservative grip on the textbook selection process in Texas was broken when liberals became sufficiently aware of it to campaign effectively for a complete overhaul of the book-selection procedures. Equal time for creation science bills made some headway until leading natural scientists realized that they could not take for granted their cultural hegemony but had to win the arguments. What any number of polls taken during Pat Robertson's campaign for Republican party presidential nominee showed was that his campaigning brought out more people who were against him than for him. And to return to the previous point, liberal anti-NCR campaigns were often very effective in labeling NCR supported candidates as single-issue people. They were also effective in preventing NCR leaders effectively deploying religious rhetoric for their "home boys" and then switching to a secular justification for a wider audience. Organizations such as People For the American Way recorded the religious rhetoric and made it widely available to audiences to which the NCR had hoped to present a very different image.

One could say a great deal more about this, but the point is a simple one. First, the majority of Americans are not Moral Majoritarians. Second, though the tendency is less marked than it is in European societies, the people who dominate the workplaces of what Berger calls the "knowledge class" (1987) are more liberal than average. Combine these observations and one concludes from logic what we have seen from experience; when those who object to the NCR are aroused to fight back, they make powerful opponents.

THE NCR AND "SECULARIZATION THEORY"

In this final section I would like to make two related points. First I will argue that Hadden (whom I will take as representative of commentators arguably over-impressed by the potential of the NCR) has been seriously misled by placing the movement in an inappropriate theoretical context (the sin which Marxists used to call "incorrectly formulating the problematic"!). Second, I will argue that correcting his mistake allows us to understand the limits to the NCR.

Wald (1990:65) says "scholars have increasingly called into question the assumption that modernization inevitably spells death for traditional religious values." Two of those scholars were Hadden and Shupe, who wrote of their "gnawing scepticism about the efficacy of secularization theory to account for all the apparent anomalies of religious influence in the modern world" (1986:xii). At about the same time as they wrote this, Hadden used his presidency of the Southern Sociological Society to author a general critique of "secularization theory" which argued that it was an ideology rather than a coherent body of ideas (1987). Not withstanding the Hadden and Swann disclaimer in 1986 about NCR electoral prospects, two years later, Hadden and Shupe concluded their study of Pat Robertson by saying: "In time the conservative Christian movement has the potential to become solidified enough to 'take over the country' (1988:286).

The links between these views can be seen in Hadden's critique of secularization theory. He first finds fault with what he calls secularization theory for being a "hodgepodge of loosely employed ideas rather than a systematic theory" (1987:598). It is, of course, true that there is no one "theory" of secularization subscribed to by all of those scholars who seek to document or explain the phenomena, but it is a trivial point because it applies equally well to every orienting principle in the social sciences. One could say the same of "class analysis" or even "Marxist class analysis." Berger (1973, 1979, 1980), Wilson (1966, 1976, 1982), and Martin (1978) all have "theories" that explain some of the changes referred to as "secularization." The important point is which of these (and others), and in which respects, is more or less well-supported by reason and data. Hadden then turns to the data and demonstrates that the people of the United States, whom he rather ethnocentrically takes as paradigmatic, show an enduring interest in religion. This is a very important point, but to present only rather superficial data on American church adherence and religiosity and not address the massive evidence of the decline of interest in religion in the rest of the modern industrial world or the extremely thoughtful analyses of the changing *nature* of American religion of such scholars as Herberg (1960), Lenski (1963), Wilson, Berger, and more recently, James Hunter (1987), is a sad omission.

Hadden also offers the new religious movements of the 1970s as refuting evidence, but here, if nowhere else, his better judgment forces him to backtrack when he admits that "the significance of the new religious movements . . . may not be so much their contributions to religious pluralism in America as the fact that their presence stimulated a tremendous volume of scholarly inquiry" (1987:604).

Hadden offers a wide range of illustrations of movements and events from around the world that show that religion can in a variety of ways still affect politics. Again, one has to say that most of these examples have little or no bearing on the discussions of religion in the modern world and are not in any sense incompatible with anything argued by Berger, Wilson or Martin (see Lechner 1991).

What is demonstrably absent from Hadden's critique is any evidence that serious students of secularization hold the views imputed to them (such as suggesting that abandonment of churches is the only way in which modernization seriously affects to their detriment the power of religious organizations and ideas, or that modernization will have the same impact on dictatorial feudal monarchies as it has on democratic capitalist democracies, or that the decline of interest in the supernatural precludes the possibility that some people in largely secular societies will continue to pursue a wide range of previously deviant religious options). He recognizes that Martin has a complex and sophisticated theory of religious change and decline but says nothing more about it. He fails to cite Wilson, Berger, Herberg, Parsons or any of the other supposed villains and cites only two summaries of the literature (Dobbelaere 1984; Shiner 1967).

The problem with Hadden's caricature of secularization theory is that though he chides it for not being a coherent theory, he fails to consider the respective merits of the specific propositions of the scholars so maligned. In particular he does not appreciate the central part played in the work of Parsons, Berger, Wilson, or Martin by cultural pluralism. In cultures where all or almost all people share the same religious world view, then there is no problem in allowing religious beliefs and symbols to dominate the public arena, in having religious leaders occupy positions of political, economic or social power, of allowing religious values to inform the socialization of the next generation, or of having every aspect of life dominated by religious precepts. In terms of familiar organization categories, religion can prosper in the "church" form. Conditions of religious pluralism profoundly change that and create the possibility of considerable social conflict. What is characteristic of most modern societies is the development of a polity and a culture that minimizes those conflicts by requiring that considerable freedom (of religious preferences as much as other choices) in the private sphere be matched by restraint of particularism in the public sphere. People in modern societies are free to choose their marriage partners by denomination or sect, but they are not permitted to restrict the employment prospects or civil liberties of people whose religions they do not share or profoundly object to. The "church" is replaced as the dominant form of religion by the "sect" (where the polity and social structure permits the maintenance of subcultures), by the denomination (as religious traditions tone down their claims to unique possession of the saving truth and recognize an increasingly large number of alternatives as being equally valid), and by the "cultic milieu" (in which people acting as "sovereign consumers" select their own mixture of elements of this or that belief system, technique, or therapy).

Using the NCR as refutation of a caricatured "secularization theory" leads to an exaggeration of its influence and to neglect of the complex social and political forces that constrain it. If one begins with a view of modern social structures that pays appropriate attention to the "functional prerequisites" of culturally plural democracies, one sees a very different picture. Our societies permit (and in some places even encourage) the maintenance of distinctive religious world views and thus encourage sociomoral contests, but they also create a structure (the division of the life-world into public and private spheres) and a culture (universalism and tolerance) which of necessity restrains such contests and requires that they be fought on general universalistic ethical and public-policy principles. In modern democratic culturally plural societies, no sociomoral interest group can plausibly promote its cases on the grounds that "the Bible (or the Koran or the Book of Mormon) says so." Instead, it must argue that equity or reason or the public good says so.

One could say so much more, but I think I have done enough to show the different understanding of the NCR that one arrives at by seeing it through the lens of the central concerns of social-scientific models of the modern world instead of forcing it to play the role of refuter of misconceptions of the complex work of students of secularization. What Hadden has in common with the spokesmen of the NCR is the mistaken belief that many of those features of the modern world which it finds objectionable (in particular, the areligious nature of the public world) are either contingent or negotiable and hence could, with the right sort of political pressure, be changed. I have argued (see Bruce 1990) that much of what the NCR wants to change is a near-inevitable consequence of cultural pluralism in a democratic industrial democracy.

REFERENCES

Aikman, D. 1988. "Washington scoreboard." *Christianity Today* (Oct. 21):22-23.

Berger, P. L. 1973. *The Social Reality of Religion*. Harmondsworth, Middlesex: Penguin.

_____. 1979. *Facing up to Modernity*. Harmondsworth, Middlesex: Penguin.

_____. 1980. *The Heretical Imperative*. London: Collins.

_____. 1987. *The Capitalist Revolution*. Aldershot: Gower.

Blumer, H. 1978. "Social unrest and collective protest." *Studies in Social Interaction* 1:1-54.

Brogan, P. 1991. "Abortion issue returns to muddy the political and legal waters." *Glasgow Herald* (Jul. 27):9.

Bruce, S. 1985. *No Pope of Rome*. Edinburgh: Mainstream.

_____. 1986. "Protestantism and politics in Scotland and Ulster," pp. 410-29 in J. K. Hadden and A. Shupe (eds.), *Prophetic Religions and Politics*. New York: Paragon House.

_____. 1988. *The Rise and Fall of the New Christian Right*. Oxford: Oxford University Press.

_____. 1990. "Modernity and fundamentalism." *British Journal of Sociology* 41:477-96.

Conway, F. and J. Siegelman. 1982. *Holy Terror*. New York: Doubleday.

Dobbelaere, K. 1984. "Secularization theories and sociological paradigms." *Social Compass* 31:199-219.

Garvey, J. H. 1993. "Fundamentalism and American law," pp. 13-27 in Marty and Appleby, *q.v.*

Gilkey, L. 1985. *Creationism on Trial*. Minneapolis: Winston Press.

Hadden, J. K. 1987. "Desacralizing secularization theory." *Social Forces* 65:587-611.

_____ and A. D. Shupe (eds.). 1986. *Prophetic Religions and Politics*. New York: Paragon House.

_____. 1988. *Televangelism*. New York: Holt.

Hadden, J. K. and C. E. Swann. 1982. *Are the Prime Time Preachers Past Their Prime?* Washington, DC: People For the American Way.

Herberg, W. 1960. *Protestant-Catholic-Jew*. Chicago: University of Chicago Press.

Hertzke, A. 1990. "Christian fundamentalists and the imperatives of American politics," pp. 67-80 in E. Sahliyeh (ed.), *Religious Resurgence and Politics in the Contemporary World*. Albany: State University of New York Press.

Hunter, J. D. 1987. *Evangelicalism*. Chicago: University of Chicago Press.

Jelen, T. G. 1987. "The effects of religious separatism on white Protestants in the 1984 presidential election." *Sociological Analysis* 48:30-45.

Johnson, S. D., J. B. Tamney, and R. Burton. 1990. "Factors influencing vote for a Christian right candidate." *Review of Religious Research* 31:291-304.

Kellstedt, L. A. 1989. "The Falwell issue agenda." *Research in the Social Scientific Study of Religion* 1:109-32.

Kelly, D. 1993. "Church, state and school boards." *USA Today* (May 4): 1.

Lechner, F. 1991. "The case against secularization." *Social Forces* 69:1103-19.

Lenski, G. 1963. *The Religious Factor*. New York: Doubleday.

McLaughlin, J. 1984. "The evangelical surge." *National Review* (Dec. 28): 20.

Martin, D. 1978. *A General Theory of Secularization*. Oxford: Blackwell.

Marty, M. and R. S. Appleby (eds.). 1991. *Fundamentalisms Observed*. Chicago: University of Chicago Press.

_____ (eds.). 1993. *Fundamentalisms and the State*. Chicago: University of Chicago Press.

PFAW. 1992. "The radical right and the 1992 election." Washington, DC: People For the American Way.

_____. 1993. "The religious right's 1993 grassroots agenda." Washington, DC: People For the American Way.

Shribman, D. 1989. "Going mainstream." *Wall Street Journal* (Sept. 26): A1, 19.

Shiner, L. 1967. "The concept of secularization in empirical research." *Journal for the Scientific Study of Religion* 6:207-20.

Smidt, C. 1988. " 'Praise the Lord' politics." *Sociological Analysis* 50:53-72.

Tamney, J. and S. D. Johnson. 1987. "Church-state relations in the eighties." *Sociological Analysis* 48:1-16.

Wald, K. D. "The new Christian right in American politics," pp. 49-65 in E. Sahliyeh (ed.), *Religious Resurgence and Politics in the Contemporary World*. Albany: State University of New York Press.

Wallis, R. and S. Bruce. 1986. "The threatened elect," pp. 261-85 in Wallis and Bruce, *Sociological Theory, Religion and Collective Action*. Belfast: Queen's University of Belfast.

_____. 1991. "Secularization." *Research in the Social Scientific Study of Religion* 3:1-31.

Weber, M. 1968. *Economy and Society*. New York: Bedminster Press.

Wilcox, C. 1986. "Evangelicals and fundamentalists in the new Christian right." *Journal for the Scientific Study of Religion* 25:355-63.

_____. 1987a. "Religious orientations and political attitudes." *American Politics Quarterly* 15:273-96.

_____. 1987b. "America's radical right revisited." *Sociological Analysis* 48:46-57.

Wilson, B. R. 1966. *Religion in Secular Society*. London: Watts.

_____. 1976. *Contemporary Transformations of Religion*. London: Oxford University Press.

_____. 1982. *Religion in Sociological Perspective*. Oxford: Oxford University Press.

2

Premillennialists at the Millennium: Some Reflections on the Christian Right in the Twenty-first Century

Clyde Wilcox
Georgetown University

Although the fundamentalist Right of the 1980s floundered on religious particularism, the Christian Coalition has sought to build bridges to Catholics, African Americans, and others. State-level organizations have recruited some politically extreme candidates for local offices, while the national organization has endorsed moderate, even moderately feminist Republicans. The organization now seems to face a major crossroads, and must decide whether to pursue moderate Republican politics, to remain a faction within the Republican party, or to try to build coalitions with morally conservative Americans who lean toward the Democratic party on nonpartisan issues.

Margaret Atwood's mid-1980s novel *The Handmaid's Tale* imagined a future world in which the Christian Right had triumphed and women were reduced to total subservience. Doctors who had performed abortions before the ascendancy of the Christian Right were executed, and women were taught that rape survivors deserved their fate because they had enticed the man.[1] Although many of the book's reviewers suggested that such an ultimate victory by the Christian Right would be extremely unlikely, others were not so sure. Some noted predictions by Marion (Pat) Robertson that conservative Christians would run America by the year 2000. Indeed, in their fundraising letters both Christian Right leaders and leaders of groups that opposed the Christian Right predicted substantial successes in the future for the Christian Right.[2]

Of course, social scientists have also at times predicted success for the Christian Right. Some sociologists predicted in early 1988 that Robertson would

---

[1] Atwood was not the only writer to imagine an America ruled by the Christian Right. Elgin (1984) imagined that Christian conservatives enforced traditional sex roles after contact with aliens. Other writers depict Christian Right control of portions of the United States (Tepper 1988), or a future incarnation of the Christian Right contending for control (Brin 1989). Still other authors (e.g., Hogan 1991) depict alien equivalents of the Christian Right. (For an overview of the role of religion in science fiction, see Reilly 1985; Bishop 1994.)

[2] Recent direct mail solicitations from People For the American Way and Americans United for Separation of Church and State have suggested that the Christian Coalition is a juggernaut that can be stopped now only with some difficulty.

win the Republican presidential nomination. In fact, Robertson spent the largest sum in American history in pursuit of the nomination and failed to win a single primary election.[3] His campaign ultimately sent only 35 pledged delegates into the convention — the second worst dollars-to-delegates ratio since the United States began collecting good data on campaign spending in 1976. Predictions of a Robertson victory seem impossible with hindsight, but the improbable frequently occurs in politics. Las Vegas set the odds against George McGovern's bid for the Democratic nomination in 1972 at 1000:1, and Jimmy Carter's staff thought that Ronald Reagan would be the easiest Republican to beat in 1980. Predicting the political future is an enterprise that is fraught with uncertainty.

The uncertainty inherent in predicting the future of the Christian Right is evident from a quick review of the status of the Christian Right a few months after the most recent presidential elections. In early 1981, Jerry Falwell was a frequent face on television, claiming that his Moral Majority had helped deliver the 1980 presidential election to Ronald Reagan. In 1985, Falwell ranked in most surveys as one of the most unpopular men in America, and although he and other Christian Right figures had been highly visible at the Republican convention, most of the Christian Right portion of the 1980 party platform remained unfulfilled. In 1989, Falwell was disbanding a bankrupt Moral Majority, and Robertson was attempting to revitalize his *700 Club* after his drubbing in the Republican primaries. After the 1992 election, the conventional wisdom was that the visible presence of the Christian Right at the Republican convention and the strong pro-life plank in the Republican platform cost the Republicans votes (for a conflicting view, see Green 1993). Yet, Falwell is considering reassembling the Moral Majority (Balmer 1992), and Robertson's Christian Coalition is vigorously contesting school board, county commission, and internal Republican elections, and actively supporting candidates for the United States Senate and for governorships in a number of states. At each turn in its fortunes, the Christian Right has defied those who predicted its triumph or its demise.

This essay will ignore the danger inherent in such predictions, and speculate on the future of the Christian Right into the twenty-first century. The first section will provide a brief history of the Christian Right in the twentieth century. The second will focus on explanations for the ultimate failure of the Christian Right in the 1980s, and the third will consider how the Christian Coalition is currently avoiding many of the problems that plagued the Moral Majority, but some of the dilemmas the Christian Coalition faces nonetheless. The final section will provide some thoughts on the future of the Christian Right.

THE CHRISTIAN RIGHT IN THE TWENTIETH CENTURY

Three times in the twentieth century — in the 1920s, the 1950s, and the 1980s — organized groups claiming to represent fundamentalist Christians have

---

[3] Robertson won several party caucuses, where organized efforts to bring supporters to the balloting are crucial. In these low-turnout elections, Robertson's organized pentecostals swamped the less intense but far more numerous supporters of Bush and Dole. Robertson won in states as diverse as Hawaii and Washington, and probably won the initial balloting in Michigan as well.

formed and been active in the interstitial zone between religion and politics. In the 1920s, groups such as the Flying Fundamentalists lobbied state legislatures to ban the teaching of evolution and eventually agitated against communism. In the 1950s, organizations like the Christian Anti-Communism Crusade preached the perils of international and domestic communism, and lobbied against the teaching of sex education in public schools. In the 1980s, the Moral Majority and Christian Voice focused on the dangers of secular humanism in the classroom and advocated a strong military to fend off the threat of international communism.

Although these three waves of fundamentalist Christian Right activity differed in important ways (Wilcox 1992), there are also important similarities.[4] Resource mobilization theorists have emphasized the importance of sympathetic organizations in providing resources for group formation (McCarthy and Zald 1977). All three sets of fundamentalist groups were started with resources provided by fundamentalist churches. Most of the organizations of the 1920s received financial and organizational support from the World's Christian Fundamentals Association, an organization formed out of the battles between fundamentalists and moderates for control of the Protestant denominations. The anticommunist groups of the 1950s were aided by the American Council of Christian Churches, a fundamentalist group formed in the 1940s. The Moral Majority benefited from the resources of Falwell's electronic ministry and from the organizational apparatus of the Baptist Bible Fellowship. The Moral Majority and Christian Voice also benefitted from resources supplied by the secular right in an effort to mobilize evangelicals into Republican politics (Guth 1983).

Second, all three movements of the fundamentalist right stressed a combined message of educational fundamentals and anticommunism. Although the Moral Majority and the Christian Voice both had wide policy agendas, activists in the Moral Majority in Ohio were most concerned with education, and most of the organization's leadership were more committed to their state Christian schools organizations than to the Moral Majority. Anticommunism was a theme in all three waves of fundamentalist groups as well. The Ohio Moral Majority was formed after a national organizer showed a film about Soviet military power.

In the latter half of the 1980s, Pat Robertson began preparing for his presidential campaign. Where the Moral Majority was based in fundamentalist Baptist churches, Robertson's support was centered among pentecostal and charismatic Christians. Robertson raised more money than any presidential nomination candidate in history and had far more contributors than any other candidate (Brown *et al.* 1994). After the 1988 election, the Moral Majority ceased operation, and Robertson went back to his *700 Club* television station. Robertson formed the Christian Coalition, which began to build grassroots organizations across the country.

---

[4] Some have questioned my claim that there is some continuity between the various waves of fundamentalist Christian Right activity in the twentieth century. Falwell himself, however, notes the continuity between the Moral Majority and the organizations of the 1920s, which he cites as sources of inspiration.

That the Christian Right was active in the 1920s, the 1950s, and the 1980s would seem to suggest a cyclical theory of Christian Right mobilization. Ted Jelen (1991) has suggested just such a theory. He argues that religious belief remains privatized during most periods but spills over into politics whenever it becomes obvious that social groups disliked by orthodox Christians (e.g., feminists, homosexuals) become vocal and visible. These groups become more active in national politics and make gains during these quiet periods of religious privatization, which spurs organizational activity by the Christian Right. Religious activism leads to particularism as denominational differences become politicized, which leads the potential Christian Right to splinter and eventually to retreat into privatization — hence a regular cycle of activity.

It is important to note that fundamentalist Christians were not passively waiting for the second coming between the various waves of organized activity. After the anticommunist groups faded in the mid-1960s, for example, fundamentalists and pentecostals continued to build churches, to establish the televangelist ministries that enabled Christian Right leaders to reach potential followers and to establish bookstores that carried political books, newsletters, and magazines.

WHY DID THE CHRISTIAN RIGHT OF THE 1980s FAIL?

Although it raised millions of dollars and received enormous amounts of media attention, the Christian Right of the 1980s cannot be deemed a success (see also Fowler 1993). Its principal agenda remained unfulfilled after twelve years of Republican rule. Although a more conservative Supreme Court has allowed states to impose some procedural regulations on abortion and has been more supportive of public displays of Christian symbols, Reagan was more interested in enacting the agenda of the financial and foreign policy conservatives than those of the Christian Right. The few pro-life policies that he enacted by executive order were reversed by Clinton within days of his inauguration.

In 1994 abortion remains legal, and public schools cannot legally begin their days with public prayer. Homosexual groups continue to make slow, halting progress toward easing societal discrimination. Women's groups claimed victory in the "Year of the Woman" in 1992, with the election of a number of new, feminist Democratic women to Congress (Cook *et al.* 1994).

Despite this unfulfilled agenda, the organizations of the 1980s have generally disbanded or receded into obscurity. After eight years of Reagan's presidency, the Moral Majority went bankrupt. The Christian Voice was forced to discontinue its Political Action Committee and rely on financing by private organizations with vastly different religious views. Robertson lost badly to moderate Episcopalian George Bush even in Southern, largely evangelical states in which he outspent Bush 3:1, and then retreated from actively seeking elected office.

Why did the Christian Right fail? Why did it appear to rise rapidly in the early 1980s, only to disband in defeat? The answer has more to do with political institutions than with broad social forces. Mass support for the Christian Right did not surge and decline: data from the National Election Studies in 1980, 1984, and 1988 showed a relatively constant 11-15 percent of whites supported the Christian Right throughout this period.[5] There is no evidence that the public dramatically changed its mind on social issues such as abortion during this period (Cook *et al.* 1992). Press attention did surge and decline, but this reflects the importance of novelty in news stories, not changing popular support.

If support remained constant, then why did the national organizations of the Christian Right disband? The Moral Majority folded its tent because it was no longer profitable to raise money through direct mail. The organization was funded almost entirely by small donations raised by mail solicitations. While I was on the Moral Majority mailing list, I was solicited for contributions every two weeks.[6] In 1984, the organization raised $11.1 million through the mail, but by 1988 that figure had declined to $3 million.

The Moral Majority's direct mail revenues declined sharply for three reasons. First, the continued success of Republican presidential candidates made it difficult to convince the organization's contributors that their money was needed to save America. Direct mail relies on the marketing of fear (Godwin 1988). When Reagan ran in 1984 on a campaign that is was "Morning in America," this seemed to negate any urgency in the mail solicitations of the Christian Right.

Second, the market for conservative mail was becoming saturated. One conservative direct mail professional told me that "every group on the Right rented every list and prospected them. Donors were deluged with solicitations." Falwell had to compete with other, specialized groups like Focus on the Family, Concerned Women of America, and various pro-life groups, as well as anticommunist organizations. When solicitations reach a certain critical level, the direct mail professional suggested, then *all* the mail ends up in the garbage.

Finally, 1988 was a very bad year for televangelists. Jim Bakker was defrocked by the Assemblies of God because of homosexual and extramarital heterosexual behavior, Jimmy Swaggert was caught in the company of a prostitute, and Oral Roberts told his supporters that God was holding him hostage, demanding a ransom or he would be called home. Robertson was forced to settle a libel suit out of court regarding his father's influence keeping him out of military action in Korea, and it was revealed that his official biographies had doctored the date of his marriage to conceal the fact that his wife was *very* pregnant when they were finally married. Such revelations made it difficult for televangelists to raise money for their favorite political causes.

If the Moral Majority went bankrupt because its direct mail operation failed, why were they so dependent on mail? The organization initially had attempted

---

[5] The NES data do not have optimal items to measure support for the Christian Right, but they are adequate. I have defined supporters as those who rate the Moral Majority or Pat Robertson at least 10° more warmly than they rate all societal groups on average. This is a fairly liberal definition, which probably overstates actual support.

[6] My unsystematic observation is that the Moral Majority solicitations went in cycles. I made three small contributions to say on the mailing list. After each gift, the first set of letters were on homosexual rights, then education, then abortion, then feminism. Letters on defense spending and on cultural politics followed. Finally the direct mail experts apparently decided that I was a misguided liberal, and sent a letter showing Falwell with starving children in Haiti, suggesting that the Moral Majority was an organization to feed the children of the developing world.

to build grassroots organizations, first by forming state chapters and then by organizing them at the county level (Liebman 1983). A few state organizations did flourish for a time in disparate states such as Indiana, Georgia, and Alaska, but the grassroots efforts of the Moral Majority were ultimately unsuccessful.[7] The same factors that enabled the Moral Majority to establish state chapters quickly ultimately limited their success.

With only a few exceptions, the Moral Majority built its state and county organizations around pastors of the Baptist Bible Fellowship. Fellowship preachers are religious entrepreneurs, who start their own churches in their homes, eventually rent a larger space, and finally build their church. Falwell himself is one of the success stories of this type of effort, for his Thomas Road Baptist Church is one of the largest in the denomination. These entrepreneurs are also active in forming Christian schools, and were willing to form state and county Moral Majority chapters.

Yet this ready network of leaders proved unable to sustain local chapters, for two main reasons. First, their efforts were spread between their pastoral duties, building their churches, building their religious schools, and the Moral Majority. Inevitably, the Moral Majority was the least important priority. Perhaps more important, Baptist Bible Fellowship pastors are an intolerant lot. At one sermon before an organizational meeting of the Ohio Moral Majority, the preacher railed against Catholics, Methodists, pentecostals, evangelicals, and even other Baptist denominations. One Moral Majority candidate survey in a midwestern state asked candidates whether they were certain that they would go to heaven if they died that night. The follow-up question asked whether their salvation was assured by works, by faith, or by other means. Such doctrinal divisions made forging broader political coalitions difficult.

Not surprisingly, my survey of the Moral Majority membership in Ohio did not turn up many Catholic members. Indeed, more than half of the membership were members of the Baptist Bible Fellowship, a small denomination on which to build a grassroots organization. Georgianna (1989) reported that the membership of the somewhat larger Indiana Moral Majority was even more heavily concentrated among the Baptist Bible Fellowship: fully 75 percent were members of this denomination. Georgianna found no Catholic members of the Indiana Moral Majority.

In my study of the Ohio Moral Majority, I interviewed the only three county chairmen who held regular meetings at length, and discussed the membership of their county organizations. Two were members of the Baptist Bible Fellowship, and their county organizations were comprised entirely of members of that denomination. The third county chairman was a Methodist minister; his organization had the only Catholics in the entire state organization and had members in several other Protestant denominations. Yet he was unable to mobilize the membership of the Baptist Bible Fellowship churches in his county, for the Baptists did not want to mingle with Catholics and pentecostals.

---

[7] Christian Voice also formed state and county chapters, some of which survive today.

Ultimately the Moral Majority failed not because of shifting public sentiments or broad historical trends. Their grassroots efforts failed because of the intolerance and distractions of the Baptist Bible Fellowship preachers, and their direct mail fundraising failed because of political conditions and market saturation. Their potential support remained constant, suggesting that in a different political climate a profitable mail operation might resume. Indeed, Falwell's temptation to resume the Moral Majority presumably centers on the profitability of antihomosexual mail in 1993.

The failure of Robertson's presidential bid was unambiguous, yet even as he lost badly in party primaries, his supporters worked behind the scenes to seize control of state party delegations and committees. Although only 35 delegates were pledged to support him on the first ballot, he clearly had more supporters at the convention. That Robertson was forced to leave politics after this defeat is a function of American political institutions. The most obvious contrast is the state of Israel, where several minority religious parties continue to hold seats in the Knesset because of proportional representation. Robertson's vote share would doubtlessly have won him a few seats in a parliamentary system, where he would head a small religious party whose significance would depend entirely on whether its votes were needed to form a government.

Although I have argued that the Christian Right of the 1980s failed to achieve its policy goals, on one level they were part of a larger success story. The secular New Right and the Republican party lent resources to help form Christian Right groups in order to facilitate the political conversion of white, evangelical Christians to Republican politics. In 1988 and again in 1992, George Bush received a substantial majority of white evangelical votes. Although his share of the evangelical vote fell to 60 percent in 1992, this was far higher than his overall 38 percent, and was remarkable for a moderate Episcopalian running against a ticket of two Southern Baptists.

My reading of the data suggests that the Christian Right did help marginally in this minirealignment, although political issues such as abortion, defense spending, feminism, and gay rights probably would have moved many evangelicals toward the Republicans even without the formation of Christian Right organizations. The available evidence suggests that the Moral Majority appealed primarily to long-time Republican activists. The Ohio chapter of the Moral Majority had very few Democrats, and most of the people I interviewed had been Republicans all their lives.

There is some evidence that the Christian Right may also have moved some votes *away* from the Republicans. Pollsters during the 1992 presidential elections noted a growing number of formerly Republican suburban women who now identified as Democrats. Although Green (1993) has concluded that social conservatism and abortion helped Bush in 1992, my own analysis suggests a different conclusion. When those voters who were ambivalent toward both Bush and Clinton are considered, the net effect of abortion and other social issues in the

1992 election was to cost Bush approximately 2 percent of the vote.[8] As Rich Bond, former chairman of the Republican party, notes, "the Christian Right was the straw that broke the camel's back for many Republican suburban voters" (personal communication). Abramowitz (1993) also found that the abortion issue hurt Bush among pro-choice Republicans and independents, while pro-life Democrats were less likely to be aware of the candidate positions on abortion and were therefore less likely to cross party lines and vote for Bush.

My survey of contributors to the Robertson and other presidential candidates, however, suggested that the activists who contributed to the Robertson campaign included a number of more recent Republican converts (Brown et al. 1994). Approximately one in three had voted for Carter in 1976, compared with approximately 10 percent of those who gave to other Republican candidates. These activists were relatively new to political contributions. Robertson's campaign also attracted some support among Southern Democrats (Wilcox 1992). This suggests that Robertson may have brought at least a few Democrats into Republican politics.

THE CHRISTIAN RIGHT IN THE 1990s: GRASSROOTS ACTIVISM AND DILEMMAS

During the 1990s, the Christian Right has to date focused on building grassroots organizations. Several large national organizations have attempted to build state and local organizations, and have generally sought to avoid the organizational mistakes of the Moral Majority. Many, such as Focus on the Family, have strength in some states or regions but not in others. Among the grassroots oriented Christian Right organizations of the 1990s, the one that has attracted the most media attention has been the Christian Coalition, which is associated with Pat Robertson.

As I finished my book (1992) on the Christian Right in the summer of 1990, I argued that the charismatic Right of Pat Robertson had a far greater potential to build a unified Christian Right than had the fundamentalists of the Moral Majority. Where the Moral Majority impaled itself on its own religious particularism, Robertson was openly ecumenical. Harrell (1988:102-3) quotes Robertson:

> In terms of the succession of the church, I'm a Roman Catholic. As far as the majesty of worship, I'm an Episcopalian; as far as the belief in the sovereignty of God, I'm a Presbyterian; in terms of holiness, I'm a Methodist; in terms of the priesthood of believers and baptism, I'm a Baptist; in terms of the baptism of the Holy Spirit, I'm a Pentecostal. So I'm a little bit of all of them.

---

[8] Abramowitz and Green both focused on those voters who listed abortion and other social issues as among the most salient in their votes or who mentioned them as important. Yet a different set of voters may have been torn between, for example, Bush's weak domestic presidency and Clinton's lack of foreign policy experience. For these voters, social issues may have been the tie breaker, yet not mentioned as salient.

In addition, I argued that Robertson had the potential to appeal to blacks. Although my survey of African Americans in the District of Columbia showed surprising support for Robertson, I doubt if many blacks would have crossed party lines to support Robertson against a Democratic candidate.[9] Moreover, support for Robertson was highest among those who knew least about him, suggesting that as the campaign progressed and information about Robertson's conservative positions on a number of issues became more widely available, black support would have declined.

Yet Robertson made an explicit appeal for black support. He launched his campaign in an African-American inner-city community, featured blacks in his advertising, backed a black Republican candidate for the Virginia Senate nomination, and mentioned blacks in his political rhetoric (Hertzke 1992). Indeed, Robertson paid more attention to the needs and concerns of blacks than any other Republican candidate in 1988, with the possible exception of Jack Kemp.

The potential for Robertson to appeal to members of various races and Christian denominations suggests that his Christian Coalition might be able to build a truly grassroots network. The Christian Coalition has avoided the mistake of the Moral Majority of building within an established denomination, instead attracting more secular activists in an attempt to build a truly ecumenical organization. The leadership of the Christian Coalition has already showed substantial political skill, and the group may be a far more formidable organization than earlier incarnations of the Christian Right.

The Christian Coalition claims a membership of 350,000 with 750 local chapters. The organization has lobbyists in several states and in Washington, and a budget of $8-10 million. Its director, Ralph Reed, is perhaps the most politically skilled of all Christian Right strategists (Sullivan 1993). Reed is a frequent guest on television talk shows, where he routinely makes free exercise claims for the Christian Right and compares the mobilization of evangelicals through the Christian Right to the mobilization of blacks through black churches in the 1960s.

The organization's motto is "Think like Jesus . . . Fight like David . . . Lead like Moses . . . Run like Lincoln." Yet the Coalition's candidates have not quite followed Lincoln's lead, for some have run as "stealth" candidates who do not divulge their connections with the Christian Coalition until after the election. *Harpers* magazine (1993) reprinted portions of a 57-page organizational manual for the Christian Coalition distributed in Pennsylvania, which the magazine claimed contained the following advice: "You should never mention the name 'Christian Coalition' in Republican circles."

The Christian Coalition has pursued a three-pronged strategy. First, state and local activists have attempted to wrest control of local and state Republican party organizations by winning precinct and county positions, by packing party caucuses, and by attempting to elect a majority to the state committees. Second, the Christian Coalition has been active in partisan elections. It has recruited

---

[9] Mark Nuttle, campaign manager for Robertson, claimed that Robertson would win 25-30 percent of the black vote in a general election (see Hertzke 1992:146).

and supported candidates especially for county and city councils, but it has also been quite active in supporting candidates for higher office. Finally, the Coalition has attempted to win control of nonpartisan school boards. The three efforts attract different sets of activists, and quite different coalitions. The organization faces a dilemma in choosing among these three strategies, for it seems unlikely that it can successfully pursue all three.

THE CHRISTIAN COALITION IN THE REPUBLICAN PARTY

Within the Republican party, the Christian Coalition built on the precinct, county, and state party organizations that Robertson's followers controlled following the 1988 convention. Christian Coalition activists have controlled at various points Republican organizations in several states, but that control has been fleeting. In Washington, the Christian Coalition together with other local Christian Right groups won control of the party, and put together a platform that focused on witchcraft and New Age religion. The party lost badly in the 1992 general elections. In late 1992, the Christian Coalition and the Oregon Citizen's Alliance narrowly missed electing the state party chairman in Oregon in a highly emotional contest; Christian Right candidates won in other important state party slots (Egan 1992; Sullivan 1993). In Houston, two parallel party committees functioned in early 1993, one dominated by the Christian Right, the other by party moderates.

In these states and others, the Christian Coalition has forged alliances with other Christian Right groups, often locally or state based. It is unclear how much of the effort to seize state and local party organizations comes from the national Christian Coalition, but it appears at this point that most of these efforts have been the inspiration of local and state activists. The model is that of an issue insurgency in a political party, similar to that of the antiwar and feminist movements in the Democratic party in 1972.

Yet in Michigan and Georgia, the party regulars regained control but worked in coalition with the Christian Coalition. That the relationship between the Christian Right and party moderates is cooperative in some states but conflictual in others may be a function of the personalities involved, or it may be part of a more systematic pattern. In states where the relationship has been more conflictual, Christian Coalition activists have appeared to take more extreme positions and to be centered on divisive issues such as homosexual rights.[10]

The long-run prospects of a Christian Right takeover of the Republican party seem dim. The successes to date have occurred while the party regulars have been distracted. Relatively low turnout precinct, county, and other party caucuses and elections are easily dominated by groups that successfully mobilize their supporters, and when the Christian Right has run "stealth candidates," the party moderates have not been mobilized to participate. When the stakes are ob-

---

[10] One Christian Coalition activist who now heads a county Republican organization in Iowa is pushing the state committee to endorse capital punishment for homosexuals, which is not an official Christian Coalition position.

vious, however, as in the contest for head of the Oregon state party organization, the moderates do participate in force.

Moreover, the party mainstream is remarkably hostile to the Christian Right. In my survey of Republican contributors, fully one in six contributors to candidates other than Robertson rated him at 0°, the lowest possible score on a 100 point feeling thermometer. Nearly one in three rated Robertson more coolly than Dukakis, and one in four rated him below Jesse Jackson (Wilcox 1992).[11] Republican moderates have formed political organizations especially designed to fight the Christian Right for control of the party (Apple 1992).

A survey of Republican voters in January, 1993 showed a party electorate that is not supportive of Christian Right figures or goals (Fabrizio 1993). Only 2 percent of those surveyed named Pat Robertson as their choice for the 1996 nomination — a figure far behind other candidates from the 1988 field. Robertson had lower favorable ratings than did Democratic president Bill Clinton, and nearly 40 percent of Republican voters expressed unfavorable views of Robertson, higher than any other Republican in the survey.

This lack of support for Robertson himself was also echoed in the issue stance of Republican voters. Only 12 percent indicated that they were attracted to the party by its moral conservatism, and only 6 percent mentioned social issues as the most salient. Few candidates mentioned abortion or gay rights in any of their responses, and of those who did, three times as many were bothered by the party's pro-life, antihomosexual stance than supported it. Many more Republican voters supported an absolute right to choose on abortion than supported the 1980-1992 platform stance that abortion should be banned with the possible exception of saving the life of the mother.

All of this suggests that the Christian Right has little chance of gaining control of the national Republican party. They can, however, be useful coalition partners in electing Republic candidates. The Christian Coalition has engaged in this second sort of electoral activity — recruiting, endorsing, and working for candidates.

CANDIDATE SUPPORT

The Christian Coalition has recruited and supported candidates across the country for state legislative races, for county commissions, and for city councils. The activists recruited by state and local Christian Coalition groups have frequently taken quite extreme issue positions and have generally run without acknowledging their ties with the Christian Coalition. There has been no effort to catalog the successes of the Christian Coalition at this level by journalists or academics, although Morken (1993) has described the process and justification in some detail.

The Christian Coalition has been much more pragmatic in national politics, especially in Senate elections after November, 1992. Following Clinton's vic-

---

[11] The Robertson contributors, in contrast, were quite warm to other Republican candidates, including Kemp and Bush.

tory, the Coalition was very active in the Georgia Senate runoff election supporting moderate Republican Paul Coverdale against the incumbent liberal Democrat. In Texas in 1993, the Christian Coalition worked actively on behalf of Kay Bailey Hutchison, despite her moderate feminism. Hutchison received money from pro-choice groups, and favored a basic right to choose, although she also supported some state restrictions such as waiting periods and parental notification. In these low-turnout elections, the Christian Coalition endorsed the Republican candidate and attempted to mobilize supporters, but it is difficult to gauge the role of the Christian Right in these elections. Coverdale won narrowly, and probably benefitted from concerted efforts by the Christian Coalition and the right-to-life movement, but Hutchison won easily and would presumably have done so even had the Christian Coalition bypassed the election.

When the Christian Coalition works in conjunction with other Christian Right groups, they can help to forge a broader coalition. In Virginia, the Christian Coalition helped Mike Farris win the Republican nomination for Lieutenant Governor in 1993. Farris's strongest support came from Christian home-school advocates, many of whom were strong fundamentalists who could not support Robertson. Yet an interview with one of Farris's home-school supporters suggested the potential for a flexible coalition involving the Christian Coalition. One Farris delegate indicated that he could never contribute to the Christian Coalition because he disapproved of Robertson's theology, but he could support Christian Coalition political candidates, including charismatic candidates.

The Christian Coalition promised to mobilize in force behind Farris in the November general election, but in fact spent most of their political capital on behalf of the candidacy of George Allen for governor. Allen won easily, although he trailed badly early in the campaign, while Farris lost a surprisingly close election. Christian Right activists in Northern Virginia were generally critical of the role of the Christian Coalition in the campaign, arguing that they claimed credit for Allen's victory without investing many resources to help Farris.

The electoral support that the Christian Right can provide to candidates in party primaries is potentially substantial. Should the Christian Coalition endorse a secular conservative for the 1996 nomination (e.g., Kemp), they could greatly help his or her candidacy in caucus states where turnout is a premium. Yet it is unclear just how far leaders such as Robertson can go in delivering the votes of his supporters to other candidates. Robertson endorsed Bush with public enthusiasm in the 1992 election, yet only 29 percent of Robertson's 1988 contributors gave money to Bush, and fully 22 percent gave to Bush's intraparty opponent Patrick Buchanan.

In electoral politics, then, the Christian Coalition has shown evidence of principled extremism in supporting candidates with little chance of winning but who take issue positions consistent with the organization platform. In other instances, however, the Christian Coalition has shown itself capable of pragmatic accommodation with Republican moderates by supporting candidates whose positions are quite divergent from Christian Coalition policy against more liberal Democrats.

The activity of the Christian Coalition in recruiting and endorsing candidates poses an interesting dilemma for the organization. Its local activists would generally prefer to nominate candidates with relatively extreme views who would hold the line on the core issues of abortion, gay rights, and school textbooks. Its national coalition partners within the Republican party are pushing the organization to moderate its positions on abortion and gay rights, and to attempt to farm traditional Republican fiscal conservatism to its members.

The national organization appears to be adopting the second strategy. During 1993, Reed attempted to focus attention on the Clinton economic package and taxes, and to downplay social issues. Robertson and later Reed have also publicly moderated their positions on abortion. Robertson has announced that he will henceforth attempt to discourage women from having abortions, rather than attempting to mobilize the role of the state to ban them. In a paper presented at a conference in late 1993, Reed wrote that Christian conservatives want a reversal of *Roe v. Wade* and a return of abortion to state governments. Reed was quite critical of *Roe*, but a policy of states rights on abortion would allow some states to codify a basic abortion right, as many have already.

The pull between moderation and broader coalitions on the one hand, and a firm position on the core social issues and narrower coalitions on the other, is one that the Christian Coalition will need to resolve in the near future. The core activists that I have interviewed and surveyed are all strongly conservative on both social and economic issues, but social issues are far more salient. One publication by the Christian Coalition in the summer of 1993 included articles that mostly focused on economic issues and letters from members that focused mostly on gays in the military. Moreover, the broader evangelical constituency that the Christian Coalition may hope to mobilize is far more moderate on economic issues, and the blacks and Catholics that they seek to include in their broader coalition are somewhat liberal on these issues.

The activists may not need persuading to adopt conservative positions on economic issues, therefore, but the larger potential constituency may be turned off by this focus. Moreover, the activists themselves may not be motivated to spend evenings and weekends working for an organization that compromises on social issues but holds the line on a gasoline tax of less than a nickel a gallon. Elsewhere, I have reported that membership in the Moral Majority was motivated by a belief that their activism was helping fight Satan's inroads into American politics (Wilcox *et al.* 1991). It is easy to pursuade pentecostals, evangelicals, fundamentalists, and even some Catholics and black Protestants that homosexuality and abortion are part of Satan's war on America. The gasoline tax or national health insurance may be a harder sell.

On the other hand, a willingness to moderate on abortion and other issues might enable the Christian Coalition to focus on a broader agenda of values. A Christian Right that focused on a broader definition of family issues, including crime prevention, the prevention of teenaged pregnancies, and so on would potentially be a far broader coalition than the Christian Right has been able to assemble to date.

THE CHRISTIAN COALITION AND
THE POLITICS OF SCHOOL BOARDS

While some in the Christian Coalition try to gain control of Republican party organizations or work in coalition with other conservative Republicans, another part of the organization has concentrated on electing Christian Right candidates to school boards. Many of these elections are nonpartisan. The Christian Coalition has recruited and trained candidates, and worked to help them gain election. In other states, including Virginia, the Christian Coalition has worked to change the law to allow for the election of school board officials. The political coalitions involved in the school board elections are broader and in many ways more interesting than those in other Christian Coalition efforts.

The Christian Coalition has had successes across the country, most notably in San Diego and New York. The Christian Coalition took control of the San Diego school board for a time, where their members proved more moderate than might have been predicted. After two years, the Christian Coalition lost its majority on the board, although it retains considerable strength. The San Diego candidates were "stealth" candidates, although the Christian Coalition connection of some candidates was leaked to the media.

In New York, the Christian Coalition capitalized on widespread dissatisfaction with a curriculum that included books such as *Heather has Two Mommies*, which described the life of a child with two lesbian parents. In these elections, the Christian Coalition was able to forge the inclusive coalitions mentioned above, for the Catholic church distributed Christian Coalition candidate lists (Dillon 1993a; 1993b), as did the Congress on Racial Equality (CORE), a religiously-based African-American civil-rights group. Ultimately the Christian Coalition candidates won about as often as those endorsed by the liberal groups (Randolph 1993). Much closer to its home ground, however, the Christian Coalition got pounded in school board elections in Virginia Beach in April, 1994.

THE MILLENNIUM AND BEYOND:
THE FUTURE OF THE CHRISTIAN RIGHT

Mindful of the inherent capacity of political predictions to embarrass greatly those who make them, I will finally venture some thoughts on the future of the Christian Right. This future does not hinge on the distribution of public opinion on the key social issues on the Christian Right agenda. Such distributions change only gradually, and for the past several decades that change has been inevitably toward greater liberalism. The American public is more tolerant today than in the 1950s, more feminist, and more supportive of gay and abortion rights. Cohort replacement, rising levels of education, and many other factors make such a creeping liberalization likely to continue.[12] Despite this gradual lib-

---

[12] Several studies have shown that the youngest Americans are somewhat more conservative on feminist issues than those who came of age in the 1960s and 1970s (Cook 1993; Cook *et al.* 1992). Yet they are far more liberal than the oldest generations, suggesting a continued liberalization as the oldest cohorts die.

eralization on these key social issues, a basic conservatism persists on core values, especially those focusing on the family.

The fortunes of organizations of the Christian Right and its opponents are not greatly influenced by mass opinion, however, but rather depend on their ability to mobilize the faithful. Consider the pro-life and pro-choice efforts of the past two decades. Throughout this period aggregate public opinion has remained quite stable — the modal American position is to favor allowing abortion in most but not all circumstances (Cook *et al.* 1992). Between a third a forty percent of Americans generally show up as consistently pro-choice in national polls, and between five percent and ten percent oppose abortion in all circumstances. Yet the organizational fortunes of National Right-to-Life and NARAL ebbed and flowed as they found issues, Court decisions, and political candidates that would mobilize their supporters to vote the abortion issue and contribute to their organizations.

Wuthnow (1993) notes that there remain important resources for the Christian Right in the 1990s and beyond. A core of support exists for Christian Right groups and policies, although it is unlikely that a Christian Right focused on social issues can expand much beyond that base (Wilcox 1992). There remains sufficient local talent to provide leadership for organizing. Denominations, churches, and television ministries possess important resources that can aid in mobilization.

Some Christian Right groups are currently getting a good return on direct mail opposing the "radical agenda of gays and lesbians." It seems likely, however, that the funding for large, national groups will never consistently reach the levels of the early 1980s, and will ultimately decline. In part, this is because direct-mail contributions for conservative religious groups appears to be a generational, rather than a life-cycle phenomenon. Direct mail experts in Washington tell me that the average age of contributors to political groups that stress religious issues is old and getting older, and it appears that when this generation of contributors moves on to their final reward or punishment the potential for direct-mail fundraising by the Right will be greatly diminished.

The membership of many pentecostal and fundamentalist churches, on the other hand, is quite young. This suggests that instead of national, direct-mail organizations such as the Moral Majority, looser coalitions of local and regional groups are more likely. There may be greater potential for inspiring these younger conservative Christians to vote in a school board election or to run phone banks for a local Christian candidate than for inspiring them to send $25 monthly to a national organization. The real pool of volunteer talent is the women of these orthodox churches, many of whom have real political skills and interests, but who accept the religious ideology that tells them they should stay at home and rear their children. These women need a justification to become involved in projects outside the home, and political issues that at least appear to be a defense of their culture can provide such a rationale.[13]

It seems to me unlikely that the Christian Right can win control of the Republican party at the national level, and I suspect that most state party organizations will again be controlled by mainstream Republicans in the next several years.[14] The majority of party voters and activists are conservative, but they do not share the Christian Right's enthusiasm for using the authority of government to dictate private moral behavior. They are quite negative toward Christian Right candidates, who are generally unelectable in general elections in any event. They are generally pro-choice on abortion, although supportive of some restrictions. The Christian Right will remain a potent force in party politics, perhaps on the level of African Americans in the Democratic party. In the near future, it is likely that the Republican party will abandon its support for a human life amendment and attempt to appear more moderate on social issues.

The future of Christian Right support for political candidates is less certain, because the Christian Coalition has followed both a purist ideological strategy and a pragmatic, accommodating one. Neither strategy seems likely to be ultimately successful. It will be difficult to explain to newly mobilized pentecostals and fundamentalists why they should consistently support Republican moderates who support abortion and who refuse to center their campaigns around Christian Right leaders. Despite Robertson's endorsement, his contributors did not rally to help finance the campaign of George Bush. Conversely, it will be difficult to mobilize support repeatedly for purist candidates who will generally lose party primaries or badly lose general elections when they do win the nomination. After a few sound defeats, premillennialists may decide that the political world cannot be saved.

Moreover, by consistently supporting Republican candidates, the Christian Right risks alienating independent or Democratic evangelicals who may support much of the Christian Right's agenda. Although Guth (1993) is correct that the party system seems to be aligning itself in part around a religious cleavage, there remain large numbers of Democratic evangelicals who must be included if the Christian Right is to expand its support. Moreover, the consistently conservative economic message of many of the Republican candidates supported by Christian Right leaders will not always be popular. In times of economic stagnation, many evangelicals will be tempted to return to their Democratic roots. If national health insurance ultimately proves successful, it will benefit the somewhat less

---

[13] Many of the fundamentalist women active in politics in Ohio whom I interviewed in 1982 seemed indirectly to suggest such a motivation. One young woman noted that she had always wanted to be more active in politics or social groups, but had always felt that she needed to spend all of her time with her young children. When the local pro-life group informed, however, she felt that defending the life of "unborn children" was sufficiently important to justify her hiring a babysitter for several hours a week.

[14] Of course, the Republican party has alternated control by moderates and conservatives for many years, and was controlled by the Right in three nominations in my lifetime. In the cases of Goldwater and Reagan, it was a coalition of defense conservatives, economic conservatives, and religious conservatives that controlled the party.

affluent evangelicals and Catholics that constitute a potential constituency for the Christian Right.

The Christian Right has its greatest potential in mobilizing diverse constituencies in support of local (and occasionally national) moral crusades. These diverse constituencies were not welcome in the Moral Majority, and it is unlikely that they will ever come together in one political organization. Yet they need not do so, for coordinated efforts at the elite level will produce the same results. Catholics in New York did not need to attend Christian Coalition meetings to receive lists of endorsed candidates — the Catholic church distributed them. African Americans did not need to attend meetings filled with white Republicans to know which candidates opposed the curriculum — the lists were distributed by CORE.

Ralph Reed (1993), director of the Christian Coalition, foresees a loose web of interconnected local groups that will cooperate on many but not all issues. A great many local groups exist already, so the real question is whether they can consistently cooperate as in the New York school board elections. I doubt if they can. The New York curriculum was perhaps the most extreme in the country, and opposition was widespread. Short-term cooperation in New York was easy, but longer-term bridges are more difficult to build. The cultural gap between conservative Catholics and fundamentalist Baptists is a wide one, and antipathy still runs deep.

Moreover, local political activists are notoriously difficult to control. The Moral Majority was consistently embarrassed by the activities of local chapters, for those with the most extreme views are generally most willing to volunteer more of their time than more moderate members, and therefore usually end up in leadership roles. The Maryland Moral Majority spent considerable effort trying to get the state assembly to pass laws outlawing anatomically correct cookies, and succeeded only in drawing national attention to one baker on the Eastern Shore who did a short-term boom mail-order business as a result. Already several state and local Christian Coalition leaders have taken astonishingly extreme positions, and seem obsessed by the apparent increase in the prevalence of witches.[15] Such local leaders do not build stable coalitions.

Finally, if the Christian Coalition continues to pursue an electoral strategy within the Republican party, it will become increasingly difficult to work well with Catholics and African Americans. Although the Republicans have made great inroads among Catholics in the past decade, many Catholics have deep Democratic roots. Among African Americans, the Republican party is quite unpopular, and any organization associated with Republican candidates will be suspect.

In the short run, then, I predict that the Christian Right will fight for but ultimately lose control of the Republican party. It will finally become a major interest group within the party. It will continue to endorse both ideological and pragmatic candidates, but find that it cannot deliver the volunteer efforts that it

---

[15] Witchcraft is alleged in current public school curricula. In addition, at least one Christian Right activist in California charges that the United States Air Force has employed official witches.

seeks in support of the candidates, nor even deliver evangelical votes in times of economic recession. It will build bridges with other groups at the national level and form ad hoc coalitions on trigger issues. But these coalitions will not endure because of religious particularism and real political divisions between the Christian Right and other conservative Christians.

As American nears the millennium, Christian Right activity and energy will likely increase. Many will believe that the millennium portends the second coming of Christ; others will devise different prophetic schemes. If the year 2002 arrives with no apocalypse, perhaps Christian Right activity will subside for a time. But Christian Right activity has waxed and waned for most of this century, and it seems likely to come again in the twenty-first century.

REFERENCES

Abramowitz, A. 1993. "It's abortion, stupid." Paper presented at the annual meeting of the American Political Science Association, Washington, DC.

Apple, R. W. 1992. "Republicans form group to regain centrist votes." *New York Times* (Dec. 16): A24.

Atwood, M. 1987. *The Handmaid's Tale*. London: Virago.

Balmer, R. 1992. "The Moral Majority's revival." *The Arizona Daily Star* (Nov. 16): A11.

Bishop, M. 1994. *Close Encounters with the Deity*. Atlanta: Peachtree.

Brin, D. 1989. *Sundiver*. New York: Bantam.

Brown, C., Jr., L. Powell, and C. Wilcox. 1994. *Serious Money*. New York: Cambridge University Press.

Cook, E. 1993. "The generations of feminism," pp. 57-67 in L. Duke (ed.), *Women in Politics*. Englewood Cliffs, NJ: Prentice-Hall.

Cook, E., T. G. Jelen, and C. Wilcox. 1992. *Between Two Absolutes*. Boulder, CO: Westview.

Cook, E., S. Thomas, and C. Wilcox. 1994. *The Year of the Woman*. Boulder, CO: Westview.

Dillon, S. 1993a. "Catholics join bid by conservatives for school boards." *New York Times* (Apr. 16): 1.

_____. 1993b. "Fundamentalists and Catholics." *New York Times* (Apr. 17): 23.

Egan, T. 1992. "Oregon GOP faces schism over agenda of Christian right." *New York Times* (Nov. 14): 6.

Elgin, S. H. 1984. *Native Tongue*. New York: Daw.

Fabrizio. 1993. *Survey of Republican Voters*. Alexandria, VA: Fabrizio, McLaughlin & Associates.

Fowler, F. B. 1993. "The failure of the religious right," pp. 57-75 in M. Cromartie (ed.), *No Longer Exiles*. Washington, CD: Ethics and Public Policy Center.

Georgianna, S. L. 1989. *The Moral Majority and Fundamentalism*. Lewiston, NY: Mellen.

Godwin, R. K. 1988. *One Billion Dollars of Influence*. Chatham, NJ: Chatham House.

Green, J. 1993. "Religion, social issues, and the Christian right." Paper presented at Colloquium on the Religious New Right and the 1992 Campaign, Ethics and Public Policy Center, Washington, DC.

Guth, J. 1983. "The politics of the new Christian right," pp. 18-43 in A. Cigler and B. Loomis (eds.), *Interest Group Politics*. Washington, DC: CQ Press.

_____. 1993. "Religion and the party system." Paper presented at the annual meeting of the American Political Science Association, Washington, DC.

Harrell, D. E. 1988. *Pat Robertson*. San Francisco: Harper & Row.

Hertzke, A. D. 1992. *Echoes of Discontent*. Washington, DC: CQ Press.

Hogan, J. P. 1991. *Ectoverse*. New York: Del Ray.

Jelen. T. G. 1991. *The Political Mobilization of Religious Beliefs*. New York: Praeger.

Liebman, R. 1983. "Mobilizing the Moral Majority," pp. 50-75 in R. Liebman and R. Wuthnow (eds.), *The New Christian Right*. New York: Aldine.

McCarthy, J. and M. Zald. 1977. "Resource mobilization and social movements." *American Journal of Sociology* 82:1212-41.

Morken, H. 1993. "The San Diego model." Paper presented at the annual meeting of the American Political Science Association, Washington, DC.

Randolph, E. 1993. "In NY school board 'holy war,' vote is split but civics triumph." *Washington Post* (May 22): A5.

Reed, R. 1993. "What do Christian conservatives really want?" Paper presented at Colloquium on the Religious New Right and the 1992 Campaign, Ethics and Public Policy Center, Washington, DC.

Reilly, R. 1985. *The Transcendent Adventure*. Westport, CT: Greenwood.

Sullivan, R. 1993. "An army of the faithful." *New York Times Magazine* (Apr. 25): 32-44.

Tepper, S. S. 1988. *The Gate to Women's Country*. New York: Bantam.

Wilcox. C. 1992. *God's Warriors*. Baltimore, MD: Johns Hopkins University Press.

_____, T. G. Jelen, and S. Linzey. 1991. "Reluctant warriors." *Journal for the Scientific Study of Religion* 30:245-58.

Wuthnow, R. 1993. "The future of the religious right," pp. 27-47 in M. Cromartie (ed.), *No Longer Exiles*. Washington, DC: Ethics and Public Policy Center.

3

What Relates to Vote for Three Religious Categories?

Stephen D. Johnson
Ball State University

For this study, 505 residents of "Middletown" (Muncie, Indiana) were randomly selected to examine what differences there might be between Catholics, conservative Protestants, and mainline Protestants in terms of factors related to how they voted in the 1992 presidential election. Social class was found to be a major factor in how Catholics voted; conservative social issues, especially traditional family values, played an important role in how conservative Protestants voted. There were no significantly distinct factors that related to how mainline Protestants voted.

The political impact of religion has been of major concern to social scientists throughout the 1980s and into the 1990s (Guth and Green 1991; Jelen 1989; Johnson and Tamney 1986; Liebman and Wuthnow 1983; Tamney 1992; Wald 1987). One political-religious phenomenon that has been of particular focus is the Christian Right movement (Guth and Green 1991; Hadden and Shupe 1988; Johnson *et al.* 1993; Liebman and Wuthnow 1983). The questions have been whether this movement had any political influence, and if so, the kind of influence. Attention has also been given to whether the Catholic vote has changed during the 1980s (Kenski and Lockwood 1989, 1991), and the influence of the Bishop's Letters on peace and the economy (D'Antonio *et al.* 1989; Tamney and Johnson 1985; Tamney *et al.* 1988). To a lesser extent the political significance of the more politically liberal causes of mainline Protestant churches, such as fighting racism and poverty, have also been examined (Johnson and Tamney 1986).

The study reported here examined the political impact of religion during the 1992 presidential election. It dealt with the question of whether or not there were *different* social and psychological variables that related to how members of three different theological categories voted in that election. The three categories were: Catholic, conservative Protestant, and mainline Protestant.

Identifying a person as a "Catholic" is rather clear-cut. But, how does one distinguish between a person who is a member of a "conservative Protestant" versus a "mainline Protestant" church? Conservative Protestant denominations generally emphasize an evangelical or fundamentalist interpretation of the Bible and the idea that obedience to the word of God found in the Bible should be the major purpose in one's life, e.g., Southern Baptists (certainly during the 1980s). Mainline Protestants have a more critical, less literal interpretation of the Bible, and are less concerned about saving their and others' souls and more concerned about helping solve society's problems, such as equal justice for all, e.g., Episcopalians. Further, Christian Rightists could be considered a subcategory of conservative Protestants. In contrast to conservative Protestants, Christian Rightists are more extreme in their religious fundamentalism and in their political conservatism, and are much more likely to demand that political office holders and American government as a whole subscribe to their fundamentalist religious perspectives.

There have been virtually no studies which have *compared* religious denominations in terms of what factors *correlate* with how members vote, so this study examines this topic on an inductive basis (Tamney *et al*. forth). To do so, it starts with another study of the 1992 presidential election in which the same population as the one examined in this study was used, but the sample as a whole, versus a subdivided one, was analyzed (Johnson *et al*. 1993). Specifically, based on previous presidential election studies by the authors (Johnson and Tamney 1982,1985; Johnson *et al*. 1991), the 1992 study of the sample as a whole examined the relative influence on vote of the social issue of traditional family values versus the economic issue of a voter's evaluation of the state of the American economy. It was found that the state of the economy was the most important factor for the sample as whole in determining how people voted (those who thought it was bad were more likely to vote for Clinton), but a voter's position on family values did have a significant impact on how he or she voted independent of economy evaluation. (Those who were traditional were less likely to vote for Clinton.) In the study reported here the sample was subdivided into the above stated three religious categories. It further considered a number of other variables measured in the sampling in addition to the measures of traditional family values and economy evaluation in order to assess if there were differences between the three religious categories in terms of which variables were most important in determining how people voted.

METHODS

Five-hundred-five residents of the SMSA of the Lynds' (1929) "Middletown" (Muncie, Indiana) who were going to vote in the 1992 presidential election were randomly selected to be interviewed over the phone. Four-hundred-five of the respondents were selected using a random-digit-dialing technique in which the proportion of respondents in the sample with a particular telephone exchange was the same as the proportion in the population as a whole. Interviews began a week-and-a-half before the election and ended four days before the election. To conduct an anticipated in-depth analysis of Catholic views on the abortion issue, an oversampling of one hundred Catholics was obtained. This was done by acquiring the telephone numbers of all members of the three Catholic churches in Muncie and then using a systematic selection procedure to obtain respondents from each of the three churches in the same proportion as the membership represented in the total Catholic population.

The basic demographics which were measured in the interview schedule were sex, race, age, work status, household income, education, and marital status. A measure of social class was constructed by summing the number of years of formal education a person had (from 0 to 17) and a ten-category scale of household income (from a "0-$5,000" category to a "$100,000 or more" category).[1]

Basic political variables which were measured were political party preference, self-identified political ideology (from very liberal to moderate to very conservative), and which of eight issues the respondent thought was the most important issue in the 1992 presidential election. The eight issues that were listed for the latter question were taxes, reducing crime, the state of the economy, education reform, protecting the environment, abortion, health-care reform, and minority rights. Another question, which was related to the issue question, asked the respondent which of seven alternatives he or she thought was the most important problem facing our society. The seven alternatives were: eliminating the federal budget deficit, reducing health-care costs, educating the young, looking after the elderly, finding a cure for AIDS, promoting traditional family values, and improving the economy.

To assess positions on economic matters, respondents were asked their evaluation of their own economic situation, their evaluation of the American economy, and for their stands on two items measuring economic conservatism. Previous work by the authors (Johnson et al. 1991) indicated that an evaluation of the American economy as a whole was more likely to relate to how people voted in presidential elections than an evaluation of one's own economic situation (Fiorina 1981; Kinder and Kiewiet 1979). This was also true in this study in that the betas for evaluation of the American economy and of personal financial situation were .20 ($p < .001$) and .13 ($p < .01$), respectively, in a regression equation in which they were included as predictor variables, and voting for Clinton was the dependent variable. Thus, to make the analyses that follow more concise only the following measure of a respondent's evaluation of the American economy was used (although this item was significantly related to a respondent's evaluation of his own financial situation, $r = .27$, $p < .01$):

How would you judge the American economy? Would you say the American economy is in

1. excellent shape
2. good shape
3. OK shape
4. not very good shape, or
5. terrible shape

Economic conservatism was assessed by asking the respondents the extent to which they agreed or disagreed with the Likert-type statements that "The American government should guarantee a job to everyone willing to work," and that "To solve the problems of poverty and unemployment, we must create a society in which goods and services are distributed more or less equally among all people." These two measures were scored so that the more the respondent dis-

---

[1] The standard deviations for the education and income measures were approximately the same (2.17 for education, 2.37 for income). The correlation between the two measures was .26 ($p < .01$).

agreed with them, the higher the score they obtained. These scores were then added to obtain a total score on economic conservatism (ALPHA = .60).

Two basic religious measures were assessed in the survey — religious preference and church attendance (the latter along a seven-point scale from "never" to "more than once a week"). We also included a measure of ideological fundamentalism which assessed the extent to which the respondent believed the Bible is the actual word of God and should be taken literally, word for word. The three church groupings used in this study were constructed in the following way:

Catholic — simply stated they were "Catholic."

Conservative Protestant — stated they were either Lutheran (Missouri Synod), Baptist, Christian Church (not the Disciples of Christ), Church of the Nazarene, Assembly of God, Church of God, or other small sectarian-type churches.

Mainline Protestant — stated they were either Methodist, Episcopalian, Presbyterian, Lutheran (not Missouri Synod), Disciples of Christ, United Church of Christ, Church of the Brethren, Friends Church, or Unitarian-Universalist.

We also considered only *whites* in the study since black churches can be very different from white churches in terms of political attitudes and behavior (Gilpin 1990; Johnson 1986; Wilcox 1991), e.g., black religiously conservative Protestant churches are much more politically liberal than most other religiously conservative Protestant churches.

Christian Rightism was measured by two Likert-type items which asked the respondent the extent to which he or she agreed or disagreed with the statements that "America is God's chosen nation" and that "Public officials have an obligation to be directed by the moral teachings of their church." These two items were added to obtain the Christian Rightism measure (Alpha = .54).

Two traditional social issues related to a Christian Right perspective in which we were interested were abortion attitude and a traditional family values perspective. Abortion was originally going to be a major focus of the 1992 election survey, so eight measures were included in the interview schedule. Abortion attitude was assessed by asking the respondent to indicate his or her position along the following scale:

Which of the following statements best describes your opinion about abortion?

1. Abortion should never be permitted.
2. Abortion should be permitted only if the life and health of the woman is in danger.
3. Abortion should be permitted if, due to her particular situation, the woman would have difficulty in caring for the child.
4. Abortion should never be forbidden.

Respondents were also asked to indicate what they believed the position to be of Clinton, Bush, and Perot on abortion along the same scale (three different questions). Respondents were further asked the extent to which they have used the abortion issue in selecting candidates for political office, along a four-point scale from it "has been the *major* issue" to it "has been of *little or no* importance." A self-analysis of the relative importance of religious beliefs versus political beliefs in shaping their views on abortion was obtained, and how many important people in their lives had the same views about abortion as the respondent was assessed (the latter along a scale of "all," "most," "about half," "few," to "none"). Finally, the author and his colleagues (Tamney et al. 1992; Johnson et al. 1992) have found that a consistent-life-view plays a somewhat larger role in forming abortion views for Catholics than for other religious denominational groups (e.g., conservative Protestants), so we included a measure of it in the 1992 election survey. A consistent-life-view is the belief that all human life is worth preserving (Bernardin 1984), and it was assessed by asking the respondents the extent to which they thought both euthanasia and capital punishment should be eliminated.

The family values measure consisted of five items that attempted to cover the different aspects of this perspective as expressed by the Republican party during the 1992 presidential campaign (Barrett 1992; Cummings 1992; Devray 1992; Kranisk 1992; Rosenthal 1992a, 1992b). One of the items was the following:

> Should there be a law protecting homosexuals from being dismissed from their jobs as teachers in public schools?
> 1. Yes
> 2. No
> 3. Not sure[2]

The other four questions were Likert-type items in which there was a five-level response from strongly agree to strongly disagree. These four items were the following:

> It is much better for everyone involved if the man is the achiever outside the home and the woman takes care of the home and family.
>
> Americans today need to take strong steps to eliminate pornography, even if it means censoring movies, television, and magazines.
>
> A breakdown in morality is the major cause of the lawlessness we find in so many of our major cities in the United States.
>
> If a woman is unmarried and pregnant, marrying the father is the correct thing to do.

In a factor analysis of these five items, the results indicated that they all fell along a single factor. The five items were thus summed to obtain a traditional family values scale score (Alpha = .57).

Finally, in a recent study (1992), I found that a measure of how much a person felt he or she had control in his or her life related to certain types of religious behaviors, so a one-item measure of this social psychological variable was ob-

---

[2] The "2" response to this item was recoded to "3," and the "3" response was recoded "2" for the traditional family values scale; to provide the same range of scores as the other four items in the scale, the resulting score was multiplied by 5/3.

tained to see if it related to voting behavior for any of our three religious groupings.

The major dependent variable in the analyses that follow was how people voted. It was measured by a set of questions. Respondents were first asked if they were definitely going to vote in the 1992 presidential election. If so, they were asked who they were going to vote for: Bush, Clinton, Perot, or some other candidate. If they were not sure, we asked toward whom they were leaning.

RESULTS

There were no significant differences among white Catholics, conservative Protestants, and mainline Protestants in how they voted. The percentages who voted for Clinton versus Bush and Perot were 40 percent (n = 126), 36 percent (n = 121), and 43 percent (n = 104), respectively (see Table 1). There were also no significant differences between the three religious groups in party preference and political ideology.

TABLE 1

Means for Study Variables for Three Religious Groups

	Catholics	Conservative Protestants	Mainline Protestants
Clinton Vote	1.40[a]	1.36	1.43
Political Party[b]	1.93	2.00	2.05
Political Ideology[c]	3.07	3.25	3.08
Social Class Level*	19.09	17.23	18.04
Economic Conservatism	5.84	5.92	5.82
Importance of Economy	1.63[a]	1.57	1.62
Importance of Abortion or Family Values	1.15[a]	1.18	1.10
American Economy Evaluation	2.01	2.08	2.12
Traditional Family Values*	15.59	16.23	15.02
Christian Rightism	5.50	5.70	5.41
Church Attendance*	5.27	4.58	4.34
Fundamentalism*	2.09	2.43	2.13
Abortion Attitude*	2.47	2.29	2.59
Perceived Clinton vs. Bush/Perot Difference on Abortion	.72	.69	.69
Others Have Same Abortion Attitude*	3.90	4.18	3.90
Abortion Used As Criterion in Voting*	2.17	2.12	1.81
Religion as Basis for Abortion Views*	2.39	2.33	2.20
Consistent Life-view*	2.94	2.57	2.71
Control of Life	3.12	3.05	3.28

*Significant mean differences at .05-level

Notes: [a] The two digits to the right of the decimal point also indicate percentages.
  [b] Scored, 1 = Democrat, 2= Independent, 3 = Republican
  [c] The higher the score the more politically conservative.

An important demographic variable for which there was a significant difference in means was social class. Specifically, Catholics were somewhat higher in social class than mainline Protestants, and the latter were somewhat higher than conservative Protestants (see Table 1; F = 8.91, p < .01). People of higher social class are also more likely to be economic conservatives (Wolfinger et al. 1980), but there was no significant difference between the three religious groups on economic conservatism.

In terms of the two variables with which we will start our religious categories analyses, i.e., evaluation of the American economy and stand on traditional family values, there was no significant difference in means in terms of how the three religious groups evaluated the American economy (for the most part they all thought in 1992 that it was bad), but there was a significant difference in means for traditional family values. Specifically, conservative Protestants were the most traditional and mainline Protestants were the least, with Catholics in-between (see Table 1; F = 3.55, p < .05). Neither the economy nor abortion/family values was considered to be more important in the election by one religious group in comparison with another.

Conservative Protestants were much more religiously fundamentalist than the other two groups (see Table 1; the t-value for the comparison of the conservative Protestant mean with the other two means was 4.96, p < .01), and Catholics were more likely to attend church than the other two groups (t-value for the comparison of the Catholic mean with the other two means was 4.57, p < .01). Conservative Protestants scored higher on Christian Rightism than the other two groups, but the difference was not significant (t for comparison was 1.43, n.s.).

Other important significant mean differences were with respect to the abortion issue. Conservative Protestants were found to be significantly more pro-life than either Catholics or mainline Protestants (see Table 1; the t-value for the comparison of the conservative Protestant mean with the other two means was 2.28, p < .05). They were also more likely than Catholics and mainline Protestants to associate with people who shared the same position on abortion (see Table 1; t-value for comparison was 2.34, p < .05). Catholics and conservative Protestants were more likely to say they use the abortion issue in selecting political candidates and to consider their religious beliefs to be more important than their political beliefs in shaping their abortion views than was the case for mainline Protestants (see Table 1; t-values for comparisons were 2.99, p < .01 and 2.73, p < .01, respectively). Catholics were more likely than either conservative Protestants or mainline Protestants to have a consistent life-view (see Table 1; t-values for comparison was 2.50, p < .05). No one group was more likely to see Clinton as more pro-choice in comparison to both Bush and Perot than any of the other two groups.

A final comparison of means indicated that there was no significant difference in means between the three religious groups with respect to a feeling of control in one's life (see Table 1).

In the previously mentioned study of the whole sample (Johnson et al. 1993), how one evaluated the American economy and one's stand on traditional family values both played an important role in how people voted in the 1992 presidential election. For this study we examined the impact on vote of these two variables within each of the three religious categories by constructing multiple regression equations with family values and economy evaluation as predictor/independent variables and Clinton vote as the dependent variable.[3] Table 2 indicates the results.

TABLE 2

Betas for Clinton Vote with Economy Evaluation
and
Traditional Family Values for Three Groups

	Catholics	Conservative Protestants	Mainline Protestants
Economy Evaluation	-.26**	-.22*	-.29**
Traditional Family Values	-.17	-.27**	-.10

* p < .05
** p < .01

Only the evaluation of the economy had a significant independent relationship to vote for Catholics and mainline Protestants, but both holding traditional family values and evaluation of the economy had significant independent relationships with vote for conservative Protestants.[4] In two previous presidential election studies, i.e., in 1984 and 1988, measures of social traditionalism, which were similar to our family values measure, were *not* related to vote independent of economy valuation (Johnson and Tamney 1984; Johnson *et al.* 1991).

---

[3] Preliminary analysis indicated that the variables considered in this study basically did not relate differently to a three-way versus a dichotomized version of the vote dependent variable. In the three-way version we measured whether our respondents were going to vote for Clinton or Bush or Perot; in the dichotomy we considered whether they picked Clinton (scored "2") versus either Bush or Perot (scored "1"). Another way of putting this is that shifts between Bush and Perot did not change significantly the impact of the independent variables on our respondents' preferences for the eventual winner of the election, Bill Clinton. To assess the main and the interaction effects on the three-way variable we used a computer routine called CHAID (Magidson 1989) which makes this assessment for crosstabulation data in which the dependent variable can be a nominal-level variable.

[4] An analysis of the sample as a whole for Clinton vote for the four categories of our abortion attitude measure showed an interesting result. Referring to this measure as described in the "Methods" section, the number 1 category was considered to be a strong pro-life position, number 2 a moderate pro-life position, number 3 a moderate pro-choice position, and number 4 a strong pro-choice position. The mean Clinton vote for these four categories, in order, were 1.46 [n = 54], 1.38 [n = 185], 1.49 [n = 61], and 1.48 [n = 114] (the two digits to the right of the decimal point also indicate a percent vote for Clinton). The implication of these results is that the abortion issue has an impact on vote only for moderate pro-lifers (the t-value for the contrast of their mean versus the three others was 2.01, p < .05). It is also the position of the greatest number of people in our study. So one could possibly argue that this is where the real battleground of the electoral battles over abortion is fought, i.e., over whether a candidate agrees or not with this more "reasonable" pro-life, or generally this more moderate, position on abortion, and not over whether or not a candidate agrees with the extremes.

Table 3 indicates the zero-order correlations between all variables analyzed in this study with Clinton vote for each of the three religious groups. Considering those variables other than the family values and economy evaluation, two variables which related to vote for Catholics but not for the other two

TABLE 3

Correlations With Clinton Vote for Three Religious Groups

	Catholics	Conservative Protestants	Mainline Protestants
Political Party	-.55**	-.53**	-.61**
Political Ideology	-.32**	-.34**	-.29**
Social Class Level	-.28**	.02	-.03
Economic Conservatism	-.24**	-.10	-.09
Importance of Economy	.09	.18*	.13
Importance of Abortion or Family Values	.02	-.23*	-.11
American Economy Evaluation	-.28**	-.25**	-.28**
Traditional Family Values	-.20**	-.28**	-.07
Christian Rightism	-.03	-.01	-.17*
Church Attendance	-.01	-.18	-.10
Fundamentalism	-.01	-.11	-.04
Abortion Attitude	.05	.03	-.08
Perceived Clinton vs. Bush/Perot Difference on Abortion	-.03	-.22**	-.01
Others Have Same Abortion Attitude	.14	-.03	-.17
Abortion Used As Criterion in Voting	-.14	-.30**	-.06
Religion as Basis for Abortion Views	-.02	-.20*	-.06
Consistent Life-view	-.10	.07	-.15
Control of Life	.02	-.25**	.05

* p < .05
** p < .01

religious groups were social class and economic conservatism (see Table 3; those of higher class and who were economic conservatives were less likely to vote for Clinton). A regression equation also indicated that class and economic conservatism were related to vote independent of economy evaluation (the only variable with a significant beta for Catholics in Table 2) and independent of each other for Catholics (betas were -.19, p < .05 for both). For conservative Protestants, the importance of both the economy and abortion/family values in the election, using the abortion issue to select candidates, concluding that religious beliefs are more important than political beliefs in forming abortion views, perceiving Clinton as more pro-choice than Bush/Perot, and a feeling of control over one's life related significantly to vote; this was not the case for the other two religious groups (see Table 3). More specifically, those who thought the abortion/family values issues were important and the economy was not used abortion in voting, concluded religious beliefs were more important than political beliefs in forming abortion views, perceived Clinton as being more pro-choice and had a feeling of control were less likely to vote for Clinton. A regression equation indicated that only using the abortion issue in voting and a feeling of control related to vote independent of family values and economy evaluation (see Table 2), and independently of each other for conservative Protestants (betas were -.27 and -.24, p < .05 for both). For mainline Protestants, those who had a Christian Right orientation were somewhat less likely to vote for Clinton, and this was not the case at all for the other two religious groups (see Table 3); but this tendency was not found to be independent of economy evaluation (the only variable with a significant beta for mainline Protestants in Table 2) in a regression analysis (beta = -.15, n.s.).

In examining those variables that independently influenced vote, which differed between the three religious categories, two could possibly be influenced by other religious factors measured in this study. They were using the abortion issue to select political candidates and traditional family values (Guth and Green 1991; Tamney 1992; Tamney *et al.* 1991). These two variables also happen to be significant only for conservative Protestants. An assessment was thus made to see which variables of all those considered in this study related to each of these two variables for conservative Protestants, but not for Catholics or mainline Protestants. Only one variable related to using abortion as a criterion in deciding on a candidate for conservative Protestants but not for Catholics or mainline Protestants, and that was considering one's religious beliefs to be more important than one's political beliefs in forming one's views about abortion (r = .24, p < .01, for conservative Protestants; and for Catholics and mainline Protestants, r = .08 and r = .14, both n.s.). Only one variable related significantly to holding traditional family values for only conservative Protestants and that was associating with people who share one's position on abortion (r = .21, p < .05, for conservative Protestants; for Catholics and mainline Protestants, r = -.05 and r = .05, both n.s.).

DISCUSSION

This study found no group differences between Catholics, conservative Protestants, and mainline Protestants in how they voted in the 1992 presidential election, or in their political party preferences or basic political ideology (see Table 1). So we might conclude that the simple denominational differences in vote or in political affiliation do not exist today as they may have existed in the past, e.g., Catholics tending to vote Democratic, Protestants tending to vote Republican (Johnstone 1992; Wuthnow 1988). However, this study did find some interesting differences in *what relates to voting* between our three religious denominational groups, and it also found some other basic descriptive differences (see Table 1) that might be used to help explain the differences in what relates to voting.

The most distinct factor that related to vote for Catholics was social class. Catholics of higher class levels and those who shared the economic perspective of the upper classes, i.e., economic conservatism, voted against Clinton, or conversely, Catholics of a more working-class level and those who were more likely to hold to the economic ideology of the working classes, i.e., economic liberalism, voted for Clinton. This same result for social class was also obtained in a separate analysis conducted by the author for Catholics versus Protestants in general for the nationwide 1991 General Social Survey data. Specifically, a similar measure of class (respondent education plus income) related to voting for Bush (vs. Dukakis) in the 1988 presidential election for Catholics, but not for Protestants.

These results for Catholics are consistent with the D'Antonio *et al.* (1989) finding that economic self-interest was the major factor influencing whether or not Catholics agreed with the generally economically liberal 1984 Pastoral Letter on the Economy (U.S. News 1984). But why was class a factor only in voting preferences for Catholics? Could it be that the impact of political events on the economic well-being of people in society is more salient in the minds of Catholics since Catholic leaders have taken a well-publicized stand on economic matters in the form of a Pastoral Letter, and this has not been the case for Protestants? Might this have led to more discussion of politics and economic status in the Catholic Church (Tamney 1992) and, in reaction, to possibly more class division in the Catholic Church in terms of what our political institutions should do in dealing with economic problems? These questions would be relevant research concerns for future study.

Turning to conservative Protestants, the finding that they were significantly more fundamentalist than the other two religious groups served as a check that our denominational classifications had some validity. The other findings for conservative Protestants rather consistently indicated that they are the ones who are mainly concerned with the politically conservative social (vs. economic) agenda advocated in the 1980s and 1990s, and that this relates to how they vote. Conservative Protestants held the most traditional family values, were the most pro-life in their abortion attitudes, and were the most likely to associate with people who had the same position on abortion. Although their abortion attitude did not relate to whom they voted for in the 1992 presidential election, those people who said the abortion issue was important in selecting a candidate voted against Clinton, who was generally seen by all three religious groups as more pro-choice than Bush and Perot (see Table 1). The similarly politically conservative social issue of traditional family values did have an independent relationship to how conservative Protestants voted, and this behavior was motivated by associating with people who shared the same views on the abortion issue for conservative Protestants.

The independent relationship between a feeling of control over one's life and voting against Bill Clinton only among conservative Protestants is difficult to explain. Conservative Protestants are generally of lower educational levels (Tamney *et al.* 1992), and this was found to be the case in this study as well (mean number of years of education for Catholics, conservative Protestants, and mainline Protestants were 13.89, 12.70, and 13.68; t-value for comparison of conservative Protestant mean with the other two means was 4.79, p < .01). People of lower educational levels are, further, less likely to be involved in politics (Flanigan and Zingale 1991). So conservative Protestants, because of their probable general lack of political involvement, are possibly less likely to have a feeling of confidence in the political arena, especially when their socially traditional issues, like abortion and family values, are not considered to be of much importance by the media, as was the case in the 1992 presidential election (Quirk and Dalager 1993). Thus, those conservative Protestants who felt they had control in their lives possibly had more political confidence to translate their generally conservative social concerns into a vote against Clinton.

A reason why the traditional family values issue played more of a role in how conservative Protestants voted for president in 1992 than it did in previous presidential elections could be that the Republican party's emphasis on the issue in the early part of the 1992 campaign gave an issue conservative Protestants had long been interested in more legitimacy (in spite of the extremes to which it was taken by some at the Republican national convention; Quirk and Dalager 1993), and this gave a group of generally politically uncertain people more confidence in using it as a basis for voting for President in 1992.

Finally, considering mainline Protestants, this study found them, based on the measures included in the study, to have no distinct characteristics which related to vote. However, we possibly did not measure the factors that would have related to how mainline Protestants voted and made them distinct.

In sum, social class divisions seem to play a distinct role in the political decision making of Catholics possibly because the relationship between economic status and political action is more a part of the discourse within the Catholic Church. The distinguishing feature of conservative Protestants is that they seem to be a major source of support for a socially conservative political theme which could possibly rival the economy in future political battles, i.e., traditional family values. Unlike the Christian Right agenda that emphasized extreme positions on abortion and other social issues and an infusion of fundamentalist religion in all aspects of life, the more religious-neutral, broader-based traditional family values, such as a need for more family discipline and sexual control, should have a broader political appeal. The conservative Protestant church could thus serve as an important organizational foundation for this new political social agenda.

REFERENCES

Barrett, P. 1992. "High court lets stand reversal of FCC bar on 'indecent material'." *Wall Street Journal* (Mar. 3):B3.

Bernardin, J. 1984. "A consistent ethic of life." *Thought* 59:99-107.

Cummings, J. 1992. "GOP women in spotlight tonight." *Atlanta Constitution* (Aug. 19):A1.

D'Antonio, W., J. Davidson, D. Hoge, and R. Wallace. 1989. *American Catholic Laity in a Changing Church*. Kansas City, MO: Sheed & Ward.

Devray, A. 1992. "Bush faults special laws for gays." *Washington Post* (Apr. 22):A14.

Fiorina, M. 1981. *Retrospective Voting in American Elections*. New Haven, CT: Yale University Press.

Flanigan, W. and N. Zingale. 1991. *Political Behavior of the American Electorate*. Washington, DC: Congressional Quarterly Press.

General Social Surveys. 1991. *Manual and Data Distributed by the Roper Center for Public Opinion Research*. Storrs: University of Connecticut.

Gilpin, W. C. 1990. *Public Faith*. St. Louis, MO: CBP Press.

Guth, J. and J. Green (eds.). 1991. *The Bible and the Ballot Box*. Boulder, CO: Westview Press.

Hadden, J. and A. Shupe. 1988. *Televangelism*. New York: Holt.

Jelen. T. (ed.). 1989. *Religion and Political Behavior in the United States*. New York: Praeger.

Johnson, S. 1986. "The role of the black church in black civil rights movements," pp. 307-24 in S. Johnson and J. Tamney, *q.v.*

_____. 1992. "The elderly and religious television." Paper presented at the North Central Sociological Association meetings. Fort Wayne, IN.

_____ and J. Tamney. 1982. "The Christian right and the 1980 presidential election." *Journal for the Scientific Study of Religion* 21:123-30.

_____. 1985. "The Christian right and the 1984 presidential election." *Review of Religious Research* 27:124-33.

_____ (eds.). 1986. *The Political Role of Religion in the United States*. Boulder, CO: Westview Press.

_____ and R. Burton. 1991. "Economic satisfaction vs. moral conservatism in the 1988 presidential election." *Sociological Focus* 19:299-314.

_____. 1992. "Pro-life and pro-choice issue voting." Paper presented at the American Political Science Association meetings, Chicago.

_____. 1993. "Family values versus economic orientation in the 1992 presidential election." Paper presented at the American Political Science Association meetings, Washington, DC.

Johnstone, R. 1992. *Religion in Society*. Englewood Cliffs, NJ: Prentice-Hall.

Kenski, H. and W. Lockwood. 1989. "The Catholic vote from 1980 to 1986," pp 109-38 in Jelen, *q.v.*

_____. 1991. "Catholic voting behavior in 1988," pp. 173-87 in Guth and Green, *q.v.*

Kinder, D. and D. Kiewiet. 1979. "Economic discontent and political behavior." *American Journal of Political Science* 23:495-527.

Kranisk, M. 1992. "Bush says he'll pay price for abortion stand." *Boston Globe* (Aug. 6):12.

Liebman, R. and R. Wuthnow (eds.). 1983. *The New Christian Right*. New York: Aldine.

Lynd, R. and H. Lynd. 1929. *Middletown*. New York: Harcourt, Brace, and World.

Magidson, J. 1989. *SPSS/PC+CHAID*. Chicago: SPSS.

Quirk, P. and J. Dalager. 1993. "The election," pp. 57-88 in M. Nelson (ed.), *The Elections in 1992*. Washington, DC: Congressional Quarterly Press.

Rosanthal, A. 1992. "Quayle says riots arose from burst of social anarchy." *New York Times* (May 20):A1.

_____. 1992b. "The politics of morality." *New York Times* (May 22):A11.

Tamney, J. 1992. *The Resilience of Christianity in the Modern World*. Albany: State University of New York Press.

Tamney, J., R. Burton, and S. Johnson. 1988. "Christianity, social class, and the Catholic bishops' economic polity." *Sociological Analysis* 49:S78-96.

Tamney, J. and S. Johnson. 1985. "Christianity and the nuclear issue." *Sociological Analysis* 46:321-27.

_____ and R. Burton. 1992. "The abortion controversy." *Journal for the Scientific Study of Religion* 31:32-46.

_____. 1994. "The abortion controversy," pp. 41-56 in T. G. Jelen and M. A. Chandler (eds.), *Abortion Politics in the United States and Canada*. New York: Praeger.

U.S. News. 1984. "U.S. bishops vs Reaganomics." *U.S. News and World Report* (Nov. 26):59.

Wald, K. 1987. *Religion and Politics in the United States*. New York: St. Martin's Press.

Wilcox, C. 1991. "Religion and electoral politics among black Americans in 1988," pp. 159-72 in Guth and Green, *q.v.*

Wolfinger, R., M. Shapiro, and F. Greenstein. 1980. *Dynamics of American Politics*. Englewood Cliffs, NJ: Prentice-Hall.

Wuthnow, R. 1988. *The Restructuring of American Religion*. Princeton, NJ: Princeton University Press.

4

Religion and Family Values in Presidential Voting

Phillip E. Hammond
University of California, Santa Barbara

Mark A. Shibley
Loyola University, Chicago

Peter M. Solow
University of Copenhagen

It is well known that ideological factors enter into the presidential voting decision. Whether such factors have impact over and beyond steering voters into one or another party is more difficult to discern, however, a dilemma complicated by the various dimensions any ideology may contain. This article looks specifically at two such dimensions in the elections of 1980, 1984, 1988, and 1992: the religious dimension and the family values dimension. In the elections of the 1980s, these two dimensions appear to have had no impact over and beyond party identification and a modest additional impact of a generalized ideological outlook. In 1992, however, both dimensions outweighed all other ideological components, with the family values dimension playing an especially potent separate role. The chapter concludes with some speculation on the implications these findings have for the two major political parties.

The term New Christian Right (NCR) has, since it came into widespread use during the past two decades, generally been understood to encompass far more than a renewal of the fundamentalist-modernist split early in this century. The Bible can still evoke bitter controversy, to be sure, but the so-called "Christian" perspective on communism, education, welfare, race relations, the criminal justice system, and — above all, perhaps — the spheres of sex and the family have in recent years been blended into the theological divide. In this essay, we assess both this blend and the amount of *separate* impact in presidential voting the various components of the NCR have had in the last four elections. We investigate specifically the separate effect of the theological aspect of the NCR (called here the Christian Right component) and the family-sexual moral aspect of the NCR (called here the Family Values component).

THE ISSUE IS JOINED

Post-election analyses aim to dissect and explain who voted for whom and for what reasons. Merely showing that persons holding attitude X voted disproportionately for candidate Y is never adequate to establish that their voting was motivated by X, however. It is usually the case that attitude X is embedded in a bundle of circumstances that would have led to a vote for Y anyway, with or without attitude X. The following Op-Ed comment, written by the first and second authors, and published on 27 September 1992, by the Santa Barbara *News Press*, illustrates how complicated it can be to make sense of voting patterns. Even there, the analysis is handicapped by the absence of party identification, however, so on the pages that follow this Op-Ed piece we try to look specifically at the role played in recent presidential elections by two different (though related) attitudes: a Christian Right perspective and a conservative Family Values perspective.

Vice Presidential candidate Al Gore's speech on September 13 at the University of Missouri was remarkably reflective of the "family values" issue.

For his largely youthful, educated audience, Gore noted that American culture is undergoing a significant revolution, and their generation is ahead of earlier generations in both recognizing the inadequacy of the old and accommodating the new. What Gore might also have said is that before the new cultural perspective gains widespread acceptance, a countering effort — often called a revitalization movement — emerges in an effort to reassert the old cultural values even as they are being replaced. This cultural tug-of-war dates back to the 1960s, of course. It picked up heat during the Reagan years, but it has emerged full-blown in this campaign. Significantly, Clinton and Gore are young enough to have grown up in the '60s and reached maturity after the Vietnam War ended. It was perhaps inevitable that this campaign thus would include sharper disagreement over moral values than we have observed in the past. Put another way, we might have expected the Republican platform to be "captured" by radical traditionalists, wanting to "revitalize" an earlier moral code, and we should not be surprised to hear Al Gore assert that today's youth are the lead generation in accepting the emerging moral code.

What may be less obvious is that "family values" is largely a repackaging of the issue that gave rise to much-noted Reagan Democrats in 1980 and '84 and thus stands to be a big factor in this election. The fact is that so-called pocketbook issues are fairly straightforward, and voters can estimate whether, in paying taxes for example, they gain or lose more than they pay. With some exceptions (for example, the Pentagon) the Republican Party since the 1930s has been the low-tax, low-spend party, and the Democrats have taxed and spent. However, there being more Americans who benefit from government expenditures than who lose, Democrats on this issue alone have an edge, especially if we note that the low-income ranks are joined by some high-income persons who agree with Justice Oliver Wendell Holmes' statement that taxes buy civilization.

Because of this Democratic advantage, therefore, Republicans must find one or more "wedge" issues to pry away sufficient numbers of otherwise Democrat-inclined voters. Nixon used anti-communism to a "silent majority," a strategy that Reagan adopted and added to by courting the religious right. In 1988, Bush inherited many of these Reagan Democrats, but developed the "morality" theme less than he did law-and-order and the containment of enemies abroad. Now in 1992, the wedge issue — in part chosen by Bush and in part thrust upon him in a Party Platform dictated by convention delegates with a traditional view of morality — has sharpened greatly. It is the combined issues of abortion, homosexuality, sex outside of marriage, and gender equality, and it is known as "family values." Will it work in this election?

As it happens, a 1988 survey of 2600 adults drawn randomly from the populations of Massachusetts, North Carolina, Ohio, and California asked about exactly these four issues, allowing a "family values index" to be constructed, ranking people from strongly supportive of the traditional morality in these four areas of behavior to strongly supportive of new morality. Males and females do not differ on this index, but age is modestly related, and in the direction Al Gore suggests; respondents his age and younger are half again as likely to support the new morality as respondents aged 60 and older. Persons in the middle age group are in between. Gore was especially correct in seeing education as facilitating rejection of the old and adoption of the new; people with college degrees are more than three times as likely to support the new morality as people who never finished high school. Theological position is also involved. People who believe that the Bible is to be taken literally (this, of course, being negatively correlated with education) are only one-fourth as likely to support the new morality as people dissenting from the inerrancy position.

But so what? Will people who might otherwise be inclined to vote Democratic instead vote Republican if they hold to the traditional morality? That, needless to say, is what George Bush is counting on by seeming to embrace a moral position he is known earlier to have rejected and that his wife rejects now.

The question is: Will it work in this campaign? A reasonable estimate might be made from the same survey. While respondents were not asked their party identification, they were asked to identify themselves politically as liberal, moderate, or conservative. We also know whether, as of October, 1988, they intended to vote for Dukakis or Bush. Let's see what influence their moral views had on their vote intention.

In 1988, among persons who regarded themselves as politically liberal, twice as many moral traditionalists (as measured by the index) declared an intention to vote for Bush as did liberals holding the newer morality. This is not a trivial number since more than a third of these self-assigned liberals were moral traditionalists, perhaps persons who, though liberal on economic matters, foreign affairs, the environment, etc., had not yet found a way to accommodate the sexual revolution of the 1960s. Just as significant, Bush lost no support from self-assigned conservatives on the moral issue; though overwhelmingly in his camp whatever their sexual moral views, those who expressed the new morality were, if anything, even stronger in their support for Bush.

But there lies the rub. In 1988 the sexual morality theme was not so starkly an issue, embedded as it was in other "social" issues such as gun control, prison leaves, and welfare payments. Today, however, the Republicans have taken the "nativist" or "revitalization" position. They claim to want to stem a cultural change that, in some fashion, is inexorable. Though involving choices, this cultural change also reflects the fact that the world has changed. The automobile and motel, for example, have made sexual encounter easier, but so too have earlier sexual maturity (by as much as three years in this century) by both males and females. This, coupled with delayed age at marriage, has greatly expanded the period of time adolescents are exposed to serious sexual conduct with serious potential consequences. The increased availability of divorce through no-fault laws is a socially engineered analog. The near disappearance of the chaperone is another.

All of this, moreover, is accompanied by an awakened sense of individual freedom — to engage sexually without regard to traditional expectations, to look upon marriage and parenthood as negotiable sources of pleasure, and — most dramatically — to regard abortion and same-sex relationships as governed by much the same individual ethic. This is a severe challenge to the sexual ethic that prevailed since at least the emergence of the middle-class in the 19th Century. Bush sees, however opaquely, that such a morality still appeals, and he has chosen it as a wedge issue in 1992. In Richard Nixon's campaign recommendation to Bush that he dump the "religious fanatics," however, is the warning that 1992 may not simply repeat 1988; erstwhile conservatives comfortable with the new morality may be more inclined to vote Democratic this time around, and erstwhile liberals may now recognize that their "liberalism" has been coopted in the name of some very intolerant ideas. Bush's "family values" tactic, in other words, is a distinct gamble.

Toward the end of this essay we will look specifically at the role played by religion and family values in the 1992 election. First, however, we take a closer look at the three preceding presidential campaigns.

IDEOLOGY AND THE POLITICAL PROCESS

American culture places great emphasis on making up one's own mind, on being independent in thought and deed. Thus, a person who has purchased five Buicks in succession will nonetheless insist that each "decision" was independently arrived at. Likewise, many life-long Democratic or Republican voters will claim to debate in their own minds at each election which candidate to favor yet consistently pull the lever of their "own" party.

Does this mean that only party identification and not ideological positions determine presidential vote? Of course not. What it does mean, however, is that ideological positions (along with such other factors as family and community allegiances) "steer" persons toward one or another party, and unless there are significant ideological shifts in the voters and/or the parties, voters' loyalties remain reasonably fixed.

Shifting of party loyalties does occur, of course, but contrary to popular perception, such shifts are unlikely to take place over a "single" issue. John F. Kennedy's Catholicism may have been an exception to this generalization, but certainly most Catholic Republicans who voted for JFK in 1960, and Protestant Democrats who voted against him, returned to their respective parties in later elections. Those that did not return contributed to a potential party realignment, but that is a phenomenon occurring on a massive scale only rarely in American political history. It is not clear whether such a realignment is occurring in late twentieth century, but claims are frequently heard that a party realignment may be taking place over the issues of religion or family values (or both).

In any discussion of the role of religion and family values in recent presidential voting, however, it is not enough to determine whether right-wing Christians or anti-abortionists voted Republican more than Democrat. It is entirely possible that such persons "always" voted Republican and would have done so again and again even if Reagan or Bush had not endorsed evangelical Protestantism and opposed abortions. As we said above, "single" issues seldom lead to a change of vote, and rarer yet do they lead to a change in party identification.

This perspective is nicely illustrated by the research of Benton Johnson and Mark A. Shibley (1989) on the role of "Christian Right" ideology in the presidential elections of 1972, 1976, and 1980. They show that persons holding Christian Right views are far more likely to hold conservative political views as well. When party affiliation is then examined, however, they find that, while the general conservative political viewpoint powerfully influences Republican Party identification, the Christian Right view point has no *independent* additional effect. Similarly, party identification itself "explains" the bulk of the presidential vote, leaving little additional impact for conservative political viewpoint to play. In their research, just as party identification "mediated" most of the effect of political ideology, so did political ideology "mediate" all of the effect of Christian Right views.

A further complexity arises, however, a point that experienced survey researchers recognize but others may not. It is bound up in what Paul F. Lazarsfeld (1958:60-67) called "the doctrine of the interchangeability of indices." The basic notion is that all measures of so-called dispositional concepts (e.g., "intelligence" as distinct from "age," "group cohesion" as distinct from "membership size") are impure. Multiple probes, with answers combined, are preferable to a single probe, therefore, but multiple probes create their own ambiguities. Take, in this instance, the notion of "conservatism." If a single question is asked in a survey (e.g., "On a scale of 1 to 10, how conservative would you say you are?"), objection can be raised that conservatism has many meanings and therefore respondents probably had different meanings in mind in answering that question. If multiple probes are used, on the other hand, it becomes apparent that, since answers are not perfectly correlated, maybe "conservatism" is not a unitary thing at all. Just as in the Graduate Record Exam, we distinguish "verbal" from "quantitative" from "analytic" skill, so may we want to distinguish economic conservatism from religious conservatism or anticommunist conservatism.

But here lies the complexity. Though verbal, quantitative, and analytic scores are not perfectly correlated, they are positively related, so questions designed to measure verbal skill will tap quantitative and analytic skill as well. Similarly, in measuring economic conservatism we are also tapping into religious conservatism, anticommunist conservatism, and so forth. Any empirical demonstration of the effect on presidential voting of either religious conservatism or family values conservatism must therefore show the *independent* effect of either or both of these factors — *over and beyond the effect of conservatism generally.* To make a homely analogy: Persons who would attribute their indigestion to the garlic in the sausage must first take into account the effects of other spicy items on the menu — for example, the onion in the salad, the paprika in the goulash, or the chili in the salsa. Perhaps any one or any combination of these is capable of producing heartburn. If so, then to diners who eat one or more of these other items, adding garlic sausage may not have additional effect. Showing that it does requires first taking into account the effect of spicy food generally, then demonstrating the *additional* effect of garlic.

When asking whether religious conservatism or family value conservatism influenced presidential voting, therefore, we are required to ask: (1) Did conservative ideology contribute to voting decisions over and beyond its role in steering people into Republican party identification? and (2) If conservative ideology did make such a contribution, was it "conservatism" generally, or did religious conservatism or conservative family values play independent roles? These questions are what we now examine.

CONSERVATIVE IDEOLOGY IN PRESIDENTIAL POLITICS

It must be conceded that no once-and-for-all definition of "conservatism" is possible. Nevertheless, for specific time periods in specific places, reasonable grasp can be made of notions of what is conservative and therefore what is liberal. An ideology of either stripe can thus be likened to an umbrella made up of multiple parts. Persons may not feel equally committed to all these component parts but may know greater comfort under one part of the umbrella than under others. Moreover, if the particular component that energizes them is singled out, they might readily accept the label "conservative" (or "liberal"), whereas they may balk at accepting such a label if it is attached to some other component. Thus the politician who calls himself a "fiscal conservative" but a "social liberal," for example.

In the late twentieth century in the United States, a number of components are believed to comprise a conservative ideology — with which the New Christian Right is often identified — even if different people emphasize different components. One component having a pedigree dating back to World War II might be labeled "anticommunism." It seems likely that the conservative "umbrella" is being reconfigured as a result of the 1989 fall of the Berlin Wall, but China, Cuba, and other entities can still trigger political sentiment. Another component, made popular by Ronald Reagan, might be called "antigovernment," a notion that taxes are too high and government bureaucracy is inefficient. A third component of conservative ideology of recent decades has been termed "law-and-order," a label that stands for favoring the death penalty, opposing gun control, and generally preferring stiffer sentences and more police presence. There is, fourth, a component that is often called the "Christian Right," an ideological position that for many decades was quite silent but since the 1970s has been increasingly outspoken. It stands for so-called Biblical values and opposes what it calls "secular humanism." Finally, and closely related to a Christian Right outlook, is a "family values" component. Many persons holding this ideological position find Biblical warrant for their views, but those views are held by many not holding a literal reading of the Protestant Bible.

More components could be added, drawn from the areas of civil rights, economic justice, immigration policy, education, and so forth. Each additional component provides further refinement of a measure of "conservatism" and the NCR, to be sure, but it does so at a diminishing return rate when it comes to social research analysis. Moreover, in secondary analysis we are limited to the use of items contained in existing survey questionnaires, so some compromises have to be expected. Items measuring the five components discussed above happen to be available, while potentially worthy items measuring other components of conservatism simply are not. We work with what we have.

Even what we have is far from what would be desirable in an ideal research project. But surveys asking about: (1) presidential vote, (2) political party affiliation, plus (3) a number of attitudes bearing on political conservatism, including religion and family values — that also extend over a range of years and thus several presidential elections — are hard to come by. Indeed, only the General Social Surveys, by the University of Chicago's National Opinion Research

Center appear to fill the bill. From them, for the presidential elections analyzed here, we have used the following questions to measure:

Presidential vote:
— Did you vote for Carter, Reagan, or Anderson (Mondale or Reagan; Dukakis or Bush; Clinton, Bush, or Perot).

Party Identification:
— Generally speaking, do you usually think of yourself as a Republican, Democrat, Independent, or what?

Anticommunist component:
— Thinking about the different kinds of governments in the world today, which of these statements comes closest to how you feel about communism as a form of government? (Choosing "It's the worst kind of all" = Anticommunism)
— Do you think our government should continue to belong to the United Nations, or should we pull out of it now? (Choosing "Pull out now" = Anticommunism)

Antigovernment component:
— We are faced with many problems in this country, none of which can be solved easily or inexpensively. I'm going to name some of these problems, and for each I'd like you to tell me whether you think we're spending too much money on it, too little, or about the right amount. {How about] on welfare? (Choosing "too much" = Antigovernment) [Half the sample was asked not about welfare spending but spending on "poor people," which elicited greater generosity.]
— Same as above but asked about "Improving conditions of Blacks." (Choosing "too much" = Antigovernment)

Law-and-Order component:
— Would you favor or oppose a law which would require a person to obtain a police permit before he or she could buy a gun? (Choosing "oppose" = Law-and-Order)
— Do you favor or oppose the death penalty for persons convicted of murder? (Choosing "Favor" = Law-and-Order)
— In general do you think courts in this area deal too harshly or not harshly enough with criminals? (Choosing "Not harshly enough" = Law-and-Order)

Christian Right component:
— The U.S. Supreme Court has ruled that no state or local government may require the reading of the Lord's Prayer or Bible verses in public schools. What are your views on this — do you approve or disapprove of the court ruling? (Choosing "Disapprove" = Christian Right)
— There are always some people whose ideas are considered bad or dangerous by other people. For instance, somebody who is against all churches and religion. If such a person wanted to make a speech in your community against churches and religion, should he be allowed to speak or not? (Choosing "Not allowed" = Christian Right)

Family Values component:
— Please tell me whether or not you think it should be possible for a pregnant woman to obtain a legal abortion if she is married and does not way any more children. (Choosing "No" = Family Values)
— There's been a lot of discussion about the way morals and attitudes about sex are changing in this country. If a man and a woman have sex relations before marriage, do you think it is always wrong, almost always wrong, wrong only sometimes, or not at all? (Choosing "Always" or "Almost always wrong" = Family Values)

— What about sexual relations between two adults of the same sex — do you think it is always wrong, almost always wrong, wrong only sometimes, or not wrong at all? (Choosing "Always" or "Almost always wrong" = Family Values)

— Do you agree or disagree with this statement? Women should take care of running their homes and leave running the country up to men. (Choosing "Agree" = Family Values)

Of course objections can be leveled against these particular indicators as being too few in number or too contaminated or too restrictive, and so on. But they are the best available, and we must use them or give up our search.

A first observation to be made is that, while the five components are clearly reflective of a conservative ideology, they are distinct from one another yet related. Table 1 shows how each component is correlated with the other four components. (For this part of our analysis, we have combined the three surveys covering the elections of 1980, 1984, and 1988.)

TABLE 1

Correlation Matrix for Components of Conservative Ideology

	Anticommunist	Antigovernment	Law-and-Order	Christian Right
Family Values	.24	insig.	.09	.47
	Anticommunist	.11	15	.24
		Antigovernment	.24	-.07
			Law-and-Order	insig.

The Anticommunist component is the only one of the five components that has significant (beyond .01) relationships with all four others. There is a surprising (though small) *negative* correlation between the Christian Right component and the Antigovernment component. And there are two correlations (between Family Values and Antigovernment, and between Law-and-Order and Christian Right) too small to reach statistical significance. What stands out, however, is the huge (by survey research standards) relationship between Family Values and Christian Right. Those two components, especially if joined by the Anticommunist component, probably "absorb" much of the conservative ideological spectrum; certainly persons scoring high on all three of these components can logically be called conservative and probably regard themselves as such.

In an important way, the above correlations make the point we made earlier — neither the NCR nor "conservatism" is a unitary thing, an ideological entity that can be measured by a single dimension. But neither are its multiple dimensions independent of one another, which means that in classifying respondents in a survey on one dimension, a researcher is also classifying them to some degree on the other dimensions. The question thus becomes (again) whether any one dimension of conservatism has some independent effect on presidential vote after the combined other dimensions of conservatism are already taken into account. This question is exactly parallel to the question that logically precedes it:

Since conservatives are more likely to be Republicans and thus vote for the Republican candidate, does conservative ideology have any independent effect on voting after party identification is already taken into account? We are now in a position to address those two questions for the elections of 1980, 1984, and 1988.

Using all of the information about voters that we discussed above — their vote, their party identification, and their scores on conservative ideology measured five different ways — we can "explain" an average of about 46 percent of the direction of vote in the three elections. The overwhelming proportion of this "explanation" is found in party identification alone; i.e., to know persons' political affiliation goes most of the way in providing whatever accuracy an observer might have in predicting their vote. But while the overwhelming proportion is provided by party identification, there is a significant contribution made by the five combined measures of conservatism over and beyond party identification. Though differing slightly from one election to the next, the strength of this independent ideological impact averages about 13 percent of the strength of party identification. Put another way, party identification has about 6.5 times the strength of "leftover" conservative ideology (as measured here) in the presidential voting in 1980, 1984, and 1988. While relatively small, therefore, conservative attitudes were significant beyond any doubt, which indicates that ideological posturing and positions on issues did play a role that went beyond the attitudinal and value forces that steered people into one or another party and kept them loyal to it.

But we have yet another question to ask: Did the kinds of conservatism described above as the Christian Right component and/or the Family Values component have any *independent* impact on presidential vote over and beyond the role played by a generalized conservative ideology? To answer that question we reanalyze the data from the three elections years pretty much as before, except this time separately by election. After assessing the impact of party identification, we look at the combination of all the components of conservative ideology minus the Christian Right component, so we can examine its separate effect. Then we put the Christian Right component back into the combination of components, and remove the Family Values component in order to see if it has separate impact. A glance at Figure 1 will help convey this process. It is as if we look at the whole "pie" with, first, the Religion (Christian Right) slice taken out and looked at separately, then we put back in the Religion slice and repeat the process but assessing this time the separate impact of Family Values. What did we find?

FIGURE 1

Components of Conservative Ideology

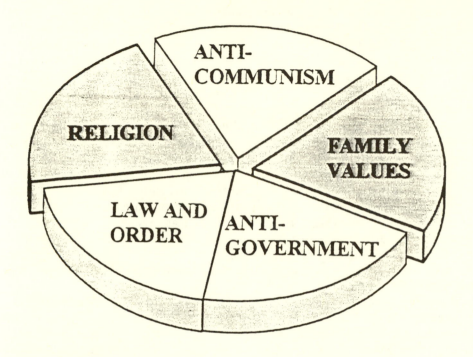

In none of the three elections did the Christian Right component have any statistically significant *additional* impact on presidential vote once party identification and an ideological measure consisting of the other components are taken into account. The Family Values component fared similarly; though it showed a statistically significant impact in the 1984 election, the impact was less than half that of the combined other four components and only one tenth the impact of party identification in that year's election.

Nor is this unexpected in light of what was earlier called the "interchangeability of indices." Following the procedure just outlined, we looked at the independent impact of each of the other three components in each election. With few exceptions, that impact was statistically insignificant, and in only one instance did a single component outweigh the combined impact of the other four, that being the role played by Antigovernment sentiment, which overwhelmed all other ideological factors in the election of Ronald Reagan in 1980.[1]

Once again, this analysis does not document the impotence of ideological factors in elections. It merely shows that after such factors help establish a party identification, there is little additional force left to expend. Similarly, once research gets a broad-gauged measure of a conservative ideology, and then assesses its impact, there is even less role to play by any particular aspect of that ideology. The question now is whether, as was widely reported in the press and elsewhere, Christian Right or Family Values conservatism had any impact in the 1992 presidential election.

THE 1992 PRESIDENTIAL VOTE

Analysis of the 1992 election data leads to nearly identical results. The total amount of voting pattern that can be "explained" is slightly less than in the combined 1980-1984-1988 analysis (40% compared with 46%). In like fashion, the interrelationships among the five ideological components shifted hardly at all from the pattern observed in Table 1. The effect of party identification on vote remains huge relative to the impact of all ideological components combined, although the independent effect of ideology in 1992 increased from 13 percent of party identification's impact in the earlier elections to 22 percent in 1992. It is in the analysis of the independent effects of the *separate* ideological components, however, that significant change is to be seen.

We noted that the Christian Right component had no additional effect in any of the three previous elections and that the Family Values component was similar; though statistically significant in 1984, its impact was still less than half that of the other four components combined. Indeed, of the 15 separate analyses possible (5 components x 3 elections), only the Antigovernment component in 1980 exceeded in impact the combined effect of the other four components. What do we find in 1992?

In the case of Anticommunism, Law-and-Order, and the Antigovernment component — looked at separately — there is no statistically significant effect over and beyond the effect of the combined other components.[2] In the case of the Christian Right and Family Values components, the situation is the reverse; each not only proved to be statistically significant, thus exhibiting an indepen-

---

[1] This "interchangeability" doctrine helps explain an apparent contradiction. The survey cited in the Op-Ed essay had claimed to find a significant role played by Family Values in the 1988 election. Why would it not show up in the General Social Survey of the same election? The answer is that the survey cited in the Op-Ed essay had no measure of party identification and only the self-assessment question to measure the conservatism-liberalism dimension. Our more refined analysis here, however, shows that any role played by Family Values in 1988 was already mediated by party identification (which was not measured at all in the other survey), and any remaining effect was essentially "absorbed" by the combined index of conservative ideology (which was inadequately measured in the other survey). The consequence was that the Family Values component had *no* statistically significant *independent* impact.

[2] Their standardized regression coefficients were .02 (in each case) compared with coefficients of .12, .09, and .10 for the combined components. The latter are significant at the .007, .003, and .02 levels.

dent effect on voting, but each also exceeded in strength the effect of the combined other components. In other words, in 1992 the religion issue and the morality issue "stood out" as the dominant components in whatever impact conservative ideology had over and beyond party identification in influencing the presidential vote.

These two issues were not equally dominant however. While the Christian Right component was 33 percent stronger than the combined other components,[3] the Family Values component was nearly *three times* as potent as *its* combined other components.[4] The suggestion is strong, therefore, that if the New Christian Right is seen as having both theological and moral aspects, it is the latter that has greater political clout. Of course, as we saw throughout all these elections, the components called above Christian Right and Family Values are strongly correlated, so it is no doubt the case that voters who are both theologically and morally conservative were especially committed to Bush in 1992. But it is just as clear that among voters who are, so to speak, conservative in one of these two ways but not both, those who are morally conservative without being on the Christian theological right were obviously more loyal to Bush than those who are on the theological right but not conservative on the moral dimension.

What does this analysis therefore say about the political impact of the New Christian Right? We offer the following generalizations:

1. While in each of the last four presidential elections, a role has been played by conservative ideology over and beyond the effect of party identification, this role has been relatively small. Moreover, apart from specifically antigovernment sentiment in 1980 and specifically religious and family value sentiment in 1992, it matters little *how* this conservative ideology was expressed and measured; any reasonable indication of conservatism was adequate to express the whole of conservative sentiments.

2. Therefore, the emergence in the 1992 vote of a NCR factor — as indexed here by the Christian Right component but especially the Family Values component — is potentially significant. While still too soon to tell, it is possible that an issue, strongly correlated with evangelical Protestant theology but primarily energized by traditional morality in the family and sexual spheres, is becoming differentiated from a more general or diffuse conservatism.

3. The long-term *political* impact of such a differentiated factor of conservatism will thus depend upon whether the two major parties continue to adopt opposing positions on the family values issue. Nixon's advice to Bush in 1992 (quoted above) is, of course, a warning to the Republican Party that it stands to lose more than it gains by promulgating the traditional morality that is being challenged on many fronts. Does it?

4. While the analysis supplied thus far shows that the family values issue played an undeniable (and undeniably separate) role in the 1992 vote, it has not

---

[3] With a standardized regression coefficient of .08 (sig. = .05) as compared with .06 (insig.).

[4] The coefficients were .11 (sig. = .01) and .04 (insig.).

indicated whether that role was one that gained Democratic votes for Bush or lost Republican votes for him — or both. On this point, the data are skimpier than we would like, but Table 2 suggests that the answer is "both." Bush lost some support from Republicans who were liberal on all the ideological dimensions, including the family values issue (read across Line 2), but Republicans who were already conservative on most of the dimensions were not influenced by their views on family values (read across Line 1). By contrast, Bush drew Democrats of both conservative and liberal stripe on the family values issue (read across Lines 3 and 4).

TABLE 2

Family Values and the 1992 Presidential Vote

Percent of Bush voters among those who are:

| | | On the Family Values Issue: | | |
	Republicans	Conservative	Moderate	Liberal
Line	On the combined other components:			
1	Conservative	78 (46)	81 (42)	— (0)
2	Liberal	81 (57)	62 (68)	70 (23)
	Democrats			
	On the combined other components:			
3	Conservative	18 (40)	7 (43)	(0) (3)
4	Liberal	15 (41)	10 (94)	4 (51)

CONCLUSION

Assuming that these four generalizations are correct, we can claim to have identified at least one of the ways by which America's "culture war" is being fought. James D. Hunter's persuasive argument (1991:42) regarding this culture war anticipated our findings:

> The divisions of political consequence today are not theological and ecclesiastical in character but the result of differing world-views. That is to say, they no longer revolve around specific doctrinal issues or styles of religious practice and organization but around our most fundamental and cherished assumptions about how to order our lives.

It would seem that of the various dimensions along which our "most fundamental and cherished assumptions" might split into liberal and conservative camps the dimension called here Family Values is the likeliest candidate. The New Christian Right, in other words, is being transformed. It is no longer fundamentalists disagreeing with modernists over biblical inerrancy but moral traditionalists alarmed over divorce, abortion, school curricula, feminism, sexual liberation, and so on. Culturally the line seems to be clearly drawn; the future political consequences of that line, however, would appear to depend upon how much that line also separates the two major parties.

REFERENCES

Hunter, J. D. 1991. *Culture Wars*. New York: Basic Books.

Johnson, B. and M. Shibley. 1989. "How new is the new Christian right?," pp. 178-98 in J. K. Hadden and A. Shupe (eds.), *Secularization and Fundamentalism Reconsidered*. New York: Paragon Press.

Lazarsfeld, P. 1959. "Problems in methodology," pp. 39-78 in R. K. Merton (ed.), *Sociology Today*. New York: Basic Books.

5

The Mood of America in the 1980s: Some Further Observations on Sociomoral Issues

John H. Simpson
University of Toronto

The entry of the New Christian Right into the American political arena in the 1980s provoked a number of scholarly controversies including a debate about the orientation of Americans to politicized sociomoral issues. Following a review of the debate, a typology of political arenas is proposed. The typology generalizes Converse's (1964) analysis of belief systems in mass publics. The hypothesis that the American political arena in the 1980s contained one of the types, a quasi-ideological politics of sociomoral issues, is tested with data from the 1980 and 1988 General Social Surveys. The hypothesis is not rejected.

While any account of American politics in the 1980s must recognize the presence of the New Christian Right in the public arena, there is much controversy about the scope and extent of its impact and importance (Bruce 1988; Moen 1989; Wilcox 1992). This chapter explores one of the controversies about so-called "Moral Majority" politics, namely, a debate about the orientation of Americans to issues that were politicized by the New Christian Right (Simpson 1983, 1988; Sigelman and Presser 1988).

Directed as it is at the problem of measuring and representing attitudes toward sociomoral issues, the debate at first glance might appear to have a limited empirical focus. The controversy, however, has implications for understanding the relationships among any set of issues in a public arena. Thus, in addition to clarifying the extent of support for sociomoral issues, this chapter is intended to enlarge our understanding of the formal properties of issue arenas in those jurisdictions where citizens' attitudes and opinions are, in some sense, factored into political decisions and public choices.

THE DEBATE

Having analyzed a number of items from the General Social Survey of 1977 (Davis and Smith 1977; hereafter GSS1977), I reported (Simpson 1983) an estimate that 30 percent of Americans were positively oriented to the "Moral Majority platform" of sociomoral issues, 42 percent were Moral Majority "fellow travellers," and the remaining portion of the population (28 percent) was liberal on these issues. Sigelman and Presser (1988) took issue with that estimate, and the debate was joined in my reply (1988) to their critique. The issue remains alive in the literature today with, for example, Hadden (1993:127) recently reporting the general tenor of my estimate, and Wilcox (1992:211-13) and Bruce (1993:63-4), following Sigelman and Presser, taking exception to it.

The debate involves three matters: (1) the choice of survey items, (2) cutting points for items, (3) the type of estimates that are made. Sigelman and Presser made a strong case that by choosing items that are oriented to *policies* and imposing strict cutting points that pit true "extremists" on the issues against the rest of the population, it is possible to show that only a very small proportion of Americans — 5 percent in 1977 — held views that could be interpreted as consistent with the positions of New Christian Right political actors. Sigelman and Presser's conclusion is based on the cross-classification of four items from GSS1977: (1) the extent to which abortion should be legal under any or only certain circumstances (ABLEGAL), (2) whether a respondent is for or against sex education in the schools (SEXEDUC), (3) attitudes toward the Equal Rights Amendment (ERA), (4) approval or disapproval of the United States Supreme Court's ruling on prayer in the schools (PRAYER).

In my reply to Sigelman and Presser, I accepted their findings and interpretation regarding the orientation of Americans to the implications of Moral Majority politics for specific *policy* outcomes as measured by the items indicated above. However, I also noted that my estimates, unlike theirs, were not point estimates and, furthermore, that my estimates did not represent an attempt to gauge orientations to *policy* matters. They were, rather, an attempt to gain a sense of the American population's orientation to certain *diffuse images and feelings* that had penetrated the American political arena and were being manipulated in pursuit of a politics of sociomoral issues. Among other things, those feelings and images had reference points in the counter-cultural life-style of the 1960s, the rise of feminism, Watergate, the outcome of the Vietnam War, and the Iran hostage incident, which indicated for some that the perceived strength of America as a nation was on the wane. As Wuthnow (1983) has pointed out, there was a blurring of the boundaries between personal morality and politics in America in the late 1970s, a blurring that made a politics of sociomoral issues possible. Those politics, for some, proceeded on the premise that the nation's stature and strength would be restored if traditional moral standards and practices were undergirded. Thus, I examined attitudes toward: (1) abortion on demand (ABANY), (2) homosexual relations between consenting adults (HOMOSEX), (3) the patriarchal breadwinner/homemaker gendered division of labor (FEFAM), (4) the ruling on school prayer (PRAYER). With the exception of PRAYER, the items examined by Sigelman and Presser and those examined by me were considerably different, and we reached different conclusions.

My estimates differed in part from those of Sigelman and Presser due to the choice of different items. They also differed because I established cutting points for items that were intended to dichotomize respondents into two camps: those whose attitudes were consistent in a broad sense with the positions of the New Christian Right (but not, necessarily, "extremist") and those who fell outside that camp. In that regard it is important to keep in mind that when respondents were surveyed by NORC in 1977 they were not filtered for orientation to the New

Christian Right. Indeed, that would have been a bit off-base in 1977. Respondents were, in other words, indicating their attitudes toward items that may not at the time have been directly connected in their minds to public and political arenas. Nevertheless, those attitudes were *in a broad sense* either consistent or inconsistent with what eventually came to be known as "Moral Majority politics." As such, they were *potential resources* for a politics of morality.

The cutting points that I imposed on the items from GSS1977 were germane to the type of estimates that I made. Those estimates were not point estimates based on marginals or the joint frequencies arising from the cross-classification of the items. Rather, my estimates were based on the *latent class analysis* of the cross-classification of the items from GSS1977: ABANY, HOMOSEX, FEFAM, and PRAYER. That analysis *tested the hypothesis* — which, in part, was based on the cutting points used to dichotomize the items — that in 1977 a putative political arena existed in the American population made up of those who were consistently liberal or conservative (but not necessarily "extremist") on the items; in other words, a two-camp political arena. As I reported (1983), the hypothesis could not be rejected. Thus, I concluded that there was a substantial basis in 1977 in the American population for a politics of sociomoral issues.

Considering subsequent events — including the presidential election campaigns of 1980, 1984, 1988, and 1992 which thematized sociomoral issues in various ways — my contention that significant attitudinal resources existed in the American population for an intense politics of sociomoral issues has, I would argue, been sustained. In the 1992 election, for example, Bush and his handlers made the calculated decision that supporting "family values" would be a resource in the political arena. Clinton took the opposite course by appealing to the gay and lesbian vote. The subsequent furor over Clinton's proposed policy regarding gays and lesbians in the armed services and the compromise outcome — "don't ask, don't tell" — highlighted the continuing salience of sociomoral issues in the American public arena.

Much water has passed under the bridge, so to speak, since 1977. Sigelman and Presser pointed out that some changes had occurred between 1977 and 1985 in the marginal distributions of the items I had examined. In particular, there were shifts in a liberal direction in response to the FEFAM and PRAYER items, while attitudes toward HOMOSEX became slightly more conservative. (The ABANY distribution was virtually the same in the two years.) Possibly significant changes over time in aggregate attitudes, the question of policies vs. image politics raised in the debate reported above, the elaboration of the relationship between latent class analysis and the typification of political arenas (Simpson, 1994b), and the existence of comparable data gathered over an interval of years suggest that the time is now ripe for a reassessment of the mood of America in the 1980s toward sociomoral issues. I begin with an exploration of the relationship between latent class analysis and the typification of political arenas.

MODELING AND TYPIFYING POLITICAL ARENAS

Latent class analysis is a technique that allows the researcher to model relations among cross-classified variables and determine whether *unmeasured* latent variables explain any observed associations. Developed by Lazarsfeld (Lazarsfeld and Henry 1968) and perfected by Goodman (1974a, b), the technique makes it possible to analyze the relations among variables that are measured at only the nominal/categorical level without violating criteria that are assumed to be met when other techniques, such as factor analysis, are used. Latent class analysis and certain related techniques (Goodman 1972a, b), then, are appealing because they allow the researcher to probe that portion of social reality that is constructed and constituted in terms of discontinuous categories: ethnicity, nationality, religion, race, gender, sexual orientation, and social class where it is conceived as "us" vs. "them" (cf. Ossowski 1963).

Moreover, in a rapidly globalizing world (Robertson and Chirico 1985; Simpson 1991; Robertson 1992) where *difference* (Bourdieu 1984) and "incommensurability and otherness" (Bernstein 1992:57-78) have become increasingly visible and contested, latent class analysis and related categorical techniques are, arguably, the methods of choice for those who wish to subject their theories about that world to empirical assessment and, of course, have the data to do so. With respect to the matter at hand, a latent class analysis of data pertaining to sociomoral issues contested in the American public arena could tell us, among other things, whether there is any truth to the assumption that there is a set of liberals and conservatives who, respectively, hold consistent positions on the issues. Conservatives and liberals would appear in the analysis as members of two distinct latent classes.

In the context of politics one thinks, naturally, of ideologically-oriented liberal and conservative camps as latent class "candidates." Thirty years ago Philip Converse, in his classic essay "The Nature of Belief Systems in Mass Publics," explicitly tied the notion of well-formulated belief systems (liberal and conservative ideological orientations) to the analysis of correlations among items measuring attitudes toward politically salient issues. Converse's analysis can be generalized into a typology of political arenas that has the desirable property of providing a guide for the detection of types of political arenas in survey data.

Among other things, Converse showed that some respondents in sample surveys of the American population had well-formed belief systems that encompassed a broad range of foreign and domestic issues, and he characterized those belief systems as "configurations of ideas and attitudes in which the elements are bound together by some form of constraint or functional interdependence" (1964:207). His operational measure of constraint was the degree of correlation among a set of items: large numbers of high correlations among diverse items indicate the presence of ideologically-based belief systems, while weak correlations suggest their absence. *Latent class analysis is an analog of factor analysis for categorical variables*. As Converse points out (1964:230), the matrix of high interitem correlations that would be observed where ideologies are present is the type of matrix that

> would be appropriate for factor analysis, the statistical technique designed to reduce a number of correlated variables to a more limited set of organizing dimensions. . . . Of course, it is the type of broad organizing dimension to be suggested by factor analysis of specific items that is usually presumed when observers discuss "ideological postures" of one sort or another.

Converse thus proposed an empirical procedure for detecting the presence (or absence) of ideologies in a set of respondents. He also showed that ideologically based belief systems were *not* widely distributed in the American population. High interitem correlations indicative of significant constraint among items measuring orientations to a wide range of domestic and foreign issues occurred among less than 20 percent of the respondents in the samples examined by Converse. He concluded that it was very difficult to attribute the political choices and actions of most individuals in mass democratic publics — at least those individuals in the mass public that formed the American electorate thirty to forty years ago — to well-developed and ideologically consistent systems of ideas, beliefs, and attitudes, since relatively few persons provided empirical evidence that they held such systems.

Converse's analysis suggested that there can be variation within a population regarding the *location* of constraint on a set of diverse issues. While not considered by Converse himself, it is the case that the *number or diversity* of salient issues can also vary. Thus, the type of politics that "bundles" together many diverse issues in opposing ideological camps can be contrasted with single-issue politics, where one policy or legislative goal mobilizes action. Taken together, variation in the diversity of salient issues and variation in the locations in a population where one would expect to find a high degree of association or constraint among measures of attitudes toward salient issues suggest a general classification scheme or typology of political arenas.

Where a political arena is characterized by *ideological politics*, an analyst would expect to find a high degree of association in the general population among a diverse set of items ranging across many problems and policies. In the case of *single issue politics*, one would expect a high degree of association among only a very limited range of items — essentially, different indicators of beliefs and attitudes toward a single issue or policy — in restricted population subgroups. Converse's *mass politics* would be characterized by high correlations among diverse items in population subgroups. High correlations, however, would not exist in the general population. Finally, *quasi-ideological politics* would be found where high correlations occur in the general population among items that are more diverse than is the case where single-issue politics hold sway. However, the items would lack the universal sweep across institutional sectors that is characteristic of beliefs and attitudes implicated in ideological politics. Figure 1 summarizes the typology.

FIGURE 1

A Typology of Political Arenas

		Issue Diversity	
		High	Low
Location of High Constraint Among Beliefs and Attitudes Toward Issues	Elites/ Subgroups	Mass Politics	Single Issue Politics
	General Population	Ideological Politics	Quasi-Ideological Politics

As is the case with any typology, Figure 1 defines logical possibilities and simplifies empirical realities. The cell entries in Figure 1 obviously do not exhaust the complexities of "actual existing politics." Nevertheless, they do provide a starting point for analysis. In the following section, I will test the hypothesis that a base existed in the American population in the 1980s for a quasi-ideological politics of sociomoral issues encompassing issues related to abortion, sexual orientation, and pornography.[1]

THE ATTITUDINAL BASE OF SOCIOMORAL POLITICS

While abortion and issues related to sexual orientation and pornography did not exhaust the interests of Moral Majority-type political action committees and lobbyists in the 1980s, it is fair to say that those matters were, clearly, among the central concerns of the politicized New Christian Right (Wilcox 1992; cf. Simpson 1994a). How did those issues fare in the general population as a basis for politics in the 1980s? Was the American population divided between those who were oriented in a liberal direction and those who were oriented in a conservative direction? In other words, was there a basis for a quasi-ideological politics of sociomoral issues? The classification "quasi-ideological" is appropriate since we will search for evidence of constraint among the issues in the general population and the range of issues is not substantively diverse, although it is broader than would be the case for single-issue politics.[2]

To test the hypothesis that there was a basis in the American population in the 1980s for a quasi-ideological politics of sociomoral issues, a latent structure analysis will be done on the cross-classification of five items from the General Social Surveys of 1980 and 1988 (Davis and Smith 1980, 1988; hereafter GSS1980, GSS1988). Data gathered in 1980 and 1988 were selected for analysis

---

[1] Further discussion and elaboration of the argument in this section is found in Simpson 1994b.

[2] Abortion, sexual orientation, and pornography do, in one sense, have a singular reference in that they refer, ultimately, to the control, use, and display of the body.

since each was a presidential election year when, arguably, the salience of socio-moral politics reached an apogee in the American political arena. The choice, furthermore, brackets the years of the Reagan presidency, when sociomoral issues emerged as a fixture in American politics. By analyzing the same items from surveys at the beginning and end of that period, change or stability over time in aggregate attitudes can be assessed.

TABLE 1

Marginal Distributions for GSS1980 and GSS1988 Items

HOMO.SEX — "What about sexual relations between two adults of the same sex — do you think it is always wrong, almost always wrong, wrong only sometimes, or not wrong at all?"

	1980		1988	
	N	%	N	%
Always Wrong	1024	69.8	720	73.7
Almost Always Wrong	84	5.7	44	4.5
Sometimes Wrong	85	5.8	53	5.4
Not Wrong At All	204	13.9	120	12.3
Other	0	0.0	0	0.0
Don't Know	68	4.6	36	3.7
No Answer	3	0.2	4	0.4

HOMO.TCH — "There are always some people whose ideas are considered bad or dangerous, for instance, a man who admits that he is a homosexual. Should such a person be allowed to teach in a college or university or not?"

	1980		1988	
	N	%	N	%
Allowed	801	54.6	552	56.5
Not Allowed	609	41.5	375	38.4
Don't Know	56	3.8	45	4.6
No Answer	2	0.1	5	0.5

ABORTANY — "Please tell me whether *you* think it should be possible for a pregnant woman to obtain a *legal* abortion if the woman wants it for any reason."

	1980		1988	
	N	%	N	%
Yes	578	39.4	338	34.6
No	828	56.4	598	61.2
Don't Know	59	4.0	37	3.8
No Answer	3	0.2	4	0.4

TABLE 1 (continued)

Marginal Distributions for GSS1980 and GSS1988 Items

PORN.LAW?   —   "Which of these statements comes closest to your feelings about pornography laws?" (1) There should be laws against the distribution of pornography whatever the age; (2) There should be laws against the distribution of pornography to persons under 18; (3) There should be no laws forbidding the distribution of pornography."

	1980		1988	
	N	%	N	%
Yes: All	591	40.3	429	43.0
Yes: <18	755	51.4	499	50.1
No Laws	90	6.1	47	4.7
Don't Know	32	2.2	19	1.9
No Answer	0	0.0	3	0.3

ATTEND   —   "How often do you attend religious services?"

	1980		1988	
	N	%	N	%
Never	167	11.4	254	17.2
Once A Year	109	7.4	108	7.3
Once or Twice a Year	230	15.7	168	11.3
Several Times A Year	223	15.2	194	13.1
Once A Month	98	6.7	116	7.8
2 To 3 Times A Month	118	8.0	143	9.7
About Weekly	91	6.2	109	7.4
Weekly	316	21.5	277	18.7
Several Times A Week	109	7.4	109	7.4
No Answer	7	0.5	3	0.2

Table 1 contains the questions and marginal distributions for five items from GSS1980 and GSS1988: HOMO.SEX, HOMO.TCH, ABORTANY, PORN.LAW?, and ATTEND. The mix of items makes it possible to probe whether support for or opposition to rights and differing moral principles are intertwined in the attitudes of Americans toward sociomoral issues. Two of the items touch on rights (HOMO.TCH. PORN.LAW?) — freedom of speech and freedom of the press. One item involves an explicit moral judgment (HOMO.SEX), and one item evokes both rights and morality (ABORTANY). ABORTANY is an item that can be interpreted as an indicator of attitudes toward granting women an absolute legal right to make the decision to abort and an indicator of attitudes toward the morality of abortion on demand where, among other things, abortion could be used in place of contraception or abstinence from sexual relations. While posing the question of legality, ABORTANY allows the respondent to "build any bridge," so to speak, to an answer, including one that may be heavily loaded with general feelings toward abortion that are not elicited by any specific or detailed reasons for favoring or opposing the legalization of abortion in particular circumstances.

The last item, ATTEND, is included in order to determine the degree of religious institutional loading on orientation to sociomoral issues. Put in Converse's terms, is participation in religion associated with constraint among beliefs and attitudes toward sociomoral issues? Clearly, the politicization of sociomoral issues in the late 1970s was fostered by some conservative religious elites. But does participation in organized religion in general tend to enhance or erode a quasi-ideological politics of sociomoral issues in America? Since the ATTEND item is included in the analysis, some insight into that question can be gained. It should be kept in mind, however, that care must be exercised in interpreting the results of the analysis. While the inclusion of ATTEND may provide some insight into the general effect of participation in religion on attitudes toward sociomoral issues, religious practice at the individual and organizational levels can and does inspire both conservative and liberal orientations to those issues. The visible tension in some mainline Protestant denominations regarding the ordination of gays and lesbians clearly underwrites the point (O'Toole et al. 1991).

Comparing the 1980 and 1988 marginals for the HOMO.SEX item there is a slight change in a conservative direction. In 1980 about 70 percent of the respondents indicated that homosexual relations between consenting adults were "always wrong." In 1988 about 74 percent of the respondents held the same view. For the HOMO.TCH item there is an even smaller difference over the period but in a liberal direction (55 vs. 57 percent). Regarding ABORTANY (abortion on demand) there is a small change in the conservative direction. In 1980, 56 percent of the respondents said "no" to abortion on demand. The percentage climbs to 61 percent in 1988. The results for PORN.LAW? change little over the period as well. In 1980 about 40 percent of the respondents were against the distribution of pornography to anyone in the population. The number climbs to 43 percent in 1988. Regarding the frequency of church attendance, 49.9 percent of the 1980 sample report that they attend church at least once a month or more. The figure for 1988 is 50.9 percent.

Regarding cutting points for the response categories of the variables in Table 1, I adhere to the strategy used in my earlier work (1983) and defended in my reply to Sigelman and Presser. That strategy divides respondents into two broad categories in terms of responses to an item: those who are liberal and those who are conservative *irrespective of the degree of liberal or conservative orientation*. The strategy, obviously, classifies the "hard-core extremists" on an issue (in either a liberal or conservative sense) together with those whose views are less extreme but are oriented in the same direction. The cutting points and relabeled categories for the items in Table 1 that are cross-classified and analyzed using the latent structure procedure are as follows: HOMO.SEX — not wrong at all, sometimes wrong, almost always wrong = liberal; always wrong = conservative. HOMO.TCH — allowed = liberal; not allowed = conservative. ABORTANY — yes = liberal; no = conservative. PORN.LAW? — no laws, yes: <18 = liberal; yes: all = conservative. The ATTEND item was dichotomized between "several times a year" and "once a month" to form the categories "infrequently" and "frequently."

FINDINGS

Table 2 contains statistics for three models testing hypotheses pertaining to the five-way cross-classification of the variables in Table 1 dichotomized as above. Model H-1 tests the hypothesis that the cell frequencies can be accounted for by the marginal distributions of the variables. That is the hypothesis of statistical independence. If it is true, there are no associations or interactions between the five variables in the cross-classification.

TABLE 2

Models Pertaining to the Cross-Classification
of the Variables in Table 2 (GSS1980 and GSS1988)

Model	LR Chi-Square	Degrees of Freedom
H-1 Independence	602.95	52
H-2 Two Latent Classes	96.91	41
H-3 Three Latent Classes	44.79	32

A model is deemed to fit the data where the ratio of chi-square to degrees of freedom is in the vicinity of 1.00. With a ratio of 11.59, H-1 does not fit the data. H-2 provides a much better fit than H-1, its ratio being 2.36. Nevertheless, H-2 does not fit the data well either. For model H-3, the ratio is 1.40. H-3 is a model that does fit the data well and is significantly different from model H-2 (chi-square is 96.91-44.79 = 52.12, with 41-32 = 9 degrees of freedom). Of the three models in Table 2, then, H-3 is the preferred model. H-3 is a test of the hypothesis that for the years 1980 and 1988 a three-class latent structure model explains the relationships between the five-way cross-classification of the variables in Table 1. Since model H-3 fits the data, the hypothesis cannot be rejected.

Before turning to a discussion of Table 3, which contains findings that provide further insight into the meaning of model H-3, I shall comment on the fact that model H-2 does not fit the data well and is rejected in favor of model H-3. Model H-2 tests the hypothesis that a two-class latent structure model explains the relationships in the five-way cross-classification of the variables in Table 1. As noted, the hypothesis can be rejected.

In my 1983 article, I reported that a two-class latent class model fit the cross-classification of the items ABANY, HOMOSEX, FEFAM, and PRAYER from GSS1977. In fact, the model fit the data very well. Applied to the cross-classification of the items HOMO.SEX, HOMO.TCH, ABORTANY, PORN.LAW?, and ATTEND from GSS1980 and GSS1988, however, a two-class latent model does not fit the data well, although a three-class model, as we have seen, does provide a good fit. Two of the items in the 1983 analysis are the same as the items included in the new analysis reported here: HOMO-

SEX/HOMO.SEX and ABANY/ABORTANY. Other items differ. Different items, different numbers of items (four in 1983, five in the present analysis) and, perhaps, different measurement years can and, in this case, do result in formally different, acceptable models. The question, then, is: To what extent do differences in acceptable models lead to substantively different conclusions? The analysis reported here suggests that the political arena for the sociomoral issues in Table 1 is somewhat more complex than the political arena for the items that were analyzed in my previous research. Nevertheless, Americans are still divided into distinct camps on the issues.

TABLE 3

Estimated Parameters for the Unrestricted, Heterogeneous
Three-Class Latent Structure Model (GSS1980 and GSS1988)

| Manifest Variables | Conditional Probabilities | | | | | |
| | 1980 Latent Class | | | 1988 Latent Class | | |
	I	II	III	I	II	III
HOMO.SEX						
LIBERAL	1.0000	.1750	.0000*	1.0000	.0000*	.0188
CONSERVATIVE	.0000*	.8250	1.0000	.0000*	1.0000	.9812
HOMO.TCH						
LIBERAL	.9996	.6176	.2112	.9102	.5448	.4081
CONSERVATIVE	.0004	.3824	.7879	.0898	.4552	.5919
ABORTANY						
LIBERAL	.7492	.4413	.1153	.7099	.4894	.0665
CONSERVATIVE	.2508	.5587	.8447	.2901	.5106	.9335
PORN.LAW?						
LIBERAL	.8687	.7921	.2098	.8690	.6411	.2706
CONSERVATIVE	.1313	.2079	.7902	.1310	.3589	.7294
ATTEND						
INFREQUENTLY	.7804	.5874	.1600	.6559	.7235	.1582
FREQUENTLY	.2196	.4126	.8400	.3441	.2765	.8418
LATENT CLASS PROBABILITIES	.0961	.2275	.1770	.1143	.1623	.2228
CONDITIONAL LATENT CLASS PROBABILITIES	.1920	.4544	.3536	.2289	.3250	.4461

*Estimated as .0000 by maximum likelihood procedure.

Table 3 contains three types of findings: conditional probabilities, latent class probabilities, and conditional latent class probabilities. The conditional probabilities indicate the probability of a respondent being at a level (liberal or conservative) on an item, given that the respondent is in a latent class (I, II, or III). For purposes of discussion, the conditional probabilities can be viewed as analogous to factor loadings in factor analysis and, hence, can be inspected with an eye to determining the nature (liberal or conservative) of the latent classes. The latent class probabilities are, simply, the estimated probabilities that a respondent is in one of the latent classes. The conditional latent class probabilities are the estimated probabilities that a respondent *in a given survey year* is in a particular latent class. The conditional latent class probabilities are handy for determining whether shifts have occurred across years in the sizes of the latent classes.

Turning first to the conditional probabilities in Table 3, one should cast an eye down the columns under the roman numerals indicating the latent classes (e.g., I). Inspecting latent class I for 1980 leads to the conclusion that it is "highly loaded" with those who are liberal on all of the issues and attend religious services infrequently. That is also true for latent class I in 1988.

Consider, next, latent class III for the two years. In each year it is loaded on those who are conservative on all of the issues and attend religious services frequently. For both years, then, latent class I contains those who tend to be consistently liberal on the issues and attend religious services infrequently, while latent class III contains those who tend to be consistently conservative on the issues and attend religious services frequently. The estimated probability (conditional latent class probability) of being liberal is .19 and .23 for 1980 and 1988, respectively. The estimated probability of being conservative is .35 (1980) and .45 (1988).

In some respects latent class II is the most interesting of the three latent classes. For both years the class is loaded on those who are conservative on HOMO.SEX, the homosexual morality item, and those who are slightly conservative on the ABORTANY item. For HOMO.TCH and PORN.LAW?, however, those in the latent class are liberal in both years, although less so in 1988 than in 1980. The pattern of loadings on latent class II, then, suggests that many Americans are somewhat conservative in terms of their moral judgments regarding sociomoral issues, but are liberal regarding the effects that the issues may have on persons' rights. In particular, respondents who fall into latent class II in both years are quite conservative regarding the morality of homosexuality. They tend to say that it is "always wrong." But they are reticent to abridge the freedom of speech of homosexuals in the post-secondary classrooms of the nation inasmuch as they tend to be liberal on the HOMO.TCH item in each of the years (less so in 1988 than in 1980). In both years members of latent class II are quite liberal on the PORN.LAW? item suggesting, perhaps, a fundamental commitment to freedom of the press. It should be noted, however, that members of the class are more liberal on the item in 1980 than they are in 1988. In both years those in latent class II tend to be infrequent attenders of religious services, more so in 1988 than in 1980. For 1980 and 1988 the estimated probability that a respondent is in latent class II is .45 and .33, respectively.

Comparing all of the conditional latent class probabilities for the two years, it would appear to be the case that the number of liberals increased very slightly over the period (.19 to .23), the number of those who held conservative moral views but were liberal on civil liberties as they are affected by the issues declined from .45 to .33, and those in the conservative camp increased from .35 to .45. It would seem, then, that the liberal camp was more or less steady over the period, and the conservatives gained some ground at the expense of the "inconsistents" in latent class II.

CONCLUSION

Based on the analysis and findings reported above, it would appear that the 1980s began with Americans divided into three camps on the sociomoral issues examined here. In 1980 about 19 percent of the respondents fell into a consistently liberal camp, while 35 percent could be classified as consistent conservatives, and 45 percent of the respondents were ambivalent. They tended to be conservative in their moral views and liberal regarding issue-related civil liberties. By 1988, the consistent liberal camp had increased slightly to about 23 percent of the respondents surveyed, the consistent conservative camp had increased to 45 percent, and the ambivalents had declined to about 33 percent. In both 1980 and 1988 there was a high probability of participation in religious services among consistent conservatives and a low probability among the consistent liberals (see the conditional probabilities in Table 3 for "attend frequently").

The findings thus suggest that the mood of America in the 1980s regarding certain sociomoral issues was a mixture of conservatism and ambivalence. As the decade began, more Americans were ambivalent as measured here than they were consistently conservative. By the last year of Reagan's presidency, that had reversed. The size of the liberal camp at both the beginning and toward the end of the decade was remarkably stable at around 20 percent of the surveyed respondents. At both the beginning and end of the decade, participation in religious services was associated with being a member of the consistently conservative camp.

Two cautions are in order. First, the general institutional conservatism detected in the analysis reported here (churchgoing at the aggregate level increases conservatism) cannot be generalized to specific individual and organizational cases. Individual religious participation and specific organizational orientations support both liberal and conservative attitudes and policies when it comes to sociomoral issues in contemporary America.

Second, the moods that exist in political arenas are precisely that — they are moods arising from the complexities of human systems of action and they are subject to the unpredictability of events in human systems of action (cf. Simpson 1992:10-12). The moods in the political arenas of advanced late capitalist democracies, then, should not be construed as mechanical determinants of political outcomes. On the contrary, they are subtle contexts or conditions within which politics proceeds. Thus, the point of the analysis reported here is not to predict whether the prospects of the New Christian Right are ebbing or flowing, but, rather, to provide some insight into the attitudinal complexion of the public arena where the New Christian Right pursued its goals in the 1980s.

REFERENCES

Bernstein, R. J. 1992. *The New Constellation*. Cambridge, MA: MIT Press.

Bourdieu, P. 1984. *A Social Critique of the Judgment of Taste*. Cambridge, MA: Harvard University Press.

Bruce, S. 1988. *The Rise and Fall of the New Christian Right*. New York: Oxford University Press.

_____. 1993. "Fundamentalism, ethnicity, and enclave," pp. 50-67 in M. E. Marty and R. S. Appleby (eds.), *Fundamentalisms and the State*. Chicago: University of Chicago Press.

Converse, P. E. 1964. "The nature of belief systems in mass publics," pp. 206-61 in D. Apter (ed.), *Ideology and Discontent*. New York: Free Press.

Davis, J. A. and T. W. Smith. 1977, 1980, 1988. *General Social Survey* (Machine-readable data file). Chicago: National Opinion Research Center.

Eliason, S. R. 1988. *The Categorical Data Analysis System Version 3.00A Users' Manual*. State College: Department of Sociology and Population Issues Research Center, Pennsylvania State University.

Goodman, L. A. 1972a. "A modified multiple regression approach to the analysis of dichotomous variables." *American Sociological Review* 37:28-46.

_____. 1972b. "A general model for the analysis of surveys." *American Journal of Sociology* 77:1035-86.

_____. 1974a. "The analysis of systems of qualitative variables when some of the variables are unobservable." *American Journal of Sociology* 79:1179-1259.

_____. 1974b. "Exploratory latent structure analysis using both identifiable and unidentifiable models." *Biometrika* 61:215-31.

Hadden, J. K. 1993. "The rise and fall of American televangelism." *Annals of the American Academy of Political and Social Science* 527:113-30.

Lazarsfeld, P. F. and N. W. Henry. 1968. *Latent Structure Analysis*. Boston: Houghton Mifflin.

Moen, M. 1989. *The Christian Right and Congress*. Tuscaloosa: University of Alabama Press.

Ossowski, S. 1963. *Class Structure in the Social Consciousness*. New York: Free Press.

O'Toole, R., D. F. Campbell, J. A. Hannigan, P. Beyer, and J. H. Simpson. 1991. "The United Church in crisis." *Studies in Religion* 10:151-63.

Robertson, R. 1992. *Globalization*. London: Sage.

_____ and J. Chirico. 1985. "Humanity, globalization, and worldwide religious resurgence." *Sociological Analysis* 46:219-59.

Sigelman, L. and S. Presser. 1988. "Measuring support for the new Christian right." *Public Opinion Quarterly* 52:325-37.

Simpson, J. H. 1983. "Moral issues and status politics." pp. 187-205 in R. Liebman and R. Wuthnow (eds.), *The New Christian Right*. New York: Aldine.

_____. 1988. "A reply to 'measuring support for the new Christian right'." *Public Opinion Quarterly* 52:338-342.

_____. 1991. "Globalization and religion," pp. 1-17 in R. Robertson and W. R. Garrett (eds.), *Religion and Global Order*. New York: Paragon.

_____. 1992. "Fundamentalism in America revisited," pp. 10-27 in B. Misztal and A. Shupe (eds.), *Religion and Politics in Comparative Perspective*. Westport, CT: Praeger.

_____. 1994a. "The body in late capitalism," pp. 1-14 in T. G. Jelen and M. A. Chandler (eds.), *Abortion Politics in the United States and Canada*. Westport, CT: Praeger.

_____. 1994b. "The structure of attitudes toward body issues in the American and Canadian populations," pp. 145-60 in T. G. Jelen and M. A. Chandler (eds.), *Abortion Politics in the United States and Canada*. Westport, CT: Praeger.

Wilcox, C. 1992. *God's Warriors*. Baltimore, MD: Johns Hopkins University Press.

Wuthnow, R. 1983. "The political rebirth of American evangelicals," pp. 167-85 in R. C. Liebman and R. Wuthnow (eds.), *The New Christian Right*. New York: Aldine.

METHODOLOGICAL NOTE

The General Social Survey is produced by the National Opinion Research Center, Chicago; tape distributed by the Roper Public Opinion Center, Storrs, Connecticut; micro diskette and codebook prepared and distributed by MicroCase Corporation, Bellevue, Washington.

The distributions reported in Table 1 and the cross-tabulations that were analyzed to fit the models and estimate the parameters that are reported in Table 2 and Table 3 were computed by the MicroCase Analysis System, created and sold by MicroCase Corporation, Bellevue, Washington (formerly Cognitive Development, Inc., Seattle). The mnemonics identifying the variables in Table 1 are from the MicroCase files for GSS1980 and GSS1988.

In 1988 the items HOMO.SEX, HOMO.TCH, ABORTANY, and PORN.LAW? were asked of two-thirds of the full GSS sample, and not all items were asked of the same two-thirds. For that reason the cross-classification of items from GSS1988 contains 430 cases. Since the test of model fit is dependent on sample size, the cross-classification of items from GSS1980 and based on 431 randomly selected cases.

The statistics and parameters reported in Table 2 and Table 3 are output from the Categorical Data Analysis System (CDAS; Eliason 1988).

6

Religious Voting Blocs in the 1992 Election: The Year of the Evangelical?*

Lyman A. Kellstedt
Wheaton College-Illinois

John C. Green
University of Akron

James L. Guth
Furman University

Corwin E. Smidt
Calvin College

   This chapter examines the political alignment and voting behavior of major American religious traditions in 1992. We discover that evangelical Protestants solidified their growing Republican proclivities of recent decades, becoming a core voting bloc within the GOP coalition. Mainline Protestants, traditionally at the center of the Republican party, deserted President Bush in large numbers for Clinton and Perot, while many Catholic voters returned to their former Democratic allegiance. The expanding bloc of secular voters provided strong additional support for Democratic candidates and liberal policies. In conclusion, we speculate on the emergence of a different kind of ethnoreligious alignment in electoral politics.

The 1992 elections were characterized by change: the defeat of an incumbent president, a strong independent candidate, upheaval in a scandal-ridden Congress, and a historic number of women elected to public office. But beneath the turmoil, more subtle changes were occurring in the basic building blocs of American electoral politics: significant alterations in the long-term connections between religious traditions and party coalitions. Indeed, because the election turned on economic problems, it provided a crucial test for the strength of ethnoreligious party alignments and for the continuing role of religion in electoral

* This chapter was originally prepared for the annual meeting of the American Political Science Association, Washington, DC, September 1-4, 1993. The authors wish to acknowledge major financial support from the Pew Charitable Trusts, which made this study possible. Additional assistance was provided by the Institute for the Study of American Evangelicals at Wheaton College, the Research and Professional Growth Committee of Furman University, the Ray C. Bliss Institute of Applied Politics at the University of Akron, and the Calvin Center for Christian Studies.

politics. And amid changes and continuities, there were harbingers of a new kind of cultural division.

Religious factors were largely ignored, however, in early accounts of the election by both journalists and scholars (Lipset 1993; Nelson 1993; Pomper 1993; Ladd 1993 is a clear exception). Preoccupied with campaign minutia and a stagnant economy, most observers missed the deeper impact of religion (Guth *et al.* 1993). The Christian Right's campaign activities were noted, of course, but primarily as tasteless and quixotic aberrations which cost George Bush some moderate votes. The voting behavior of religious groups was usually explained by reference to economic status, while the proclivities of more secular voters went unnoticed, or paradoxically, were assumed to be the social norm. Given the agenda of the mass media and the biases of social science, such interpretations are hardly surprising, but they are in need of correction nonetheless.

This chapter presents a different perspective on the election. In our view, the building blocs of contemporary American party coalitions are still ethnoreligious groups with their distinctive values. Economic questions represent, by comparison, transient forces that surge and decline within the channels provided by the cultural bedrock. Thus, we reverse the conventional wisdom on the primacy of electoral forces: cultural alignments come first, economics second. Economic issues and evaluations were indeed critical in 1992, as they often are, but the voters' response to economic stress is best understood against the baseline of fundamental cultural cleavages. Although ethnoreligious alignments have undergone substantial shifts in the past three decades, they are still the underpinning of American party politics.

Central to our argument is the political behavior of the major religious traditions in 1992. First, white evangelical Protestants solidified their support for the Republican party and replaced Protestant mainliners as the most loyal adherents to the GOP. This attachment reflects both their social traditionalism and, to a lesser extent, preferences for conservative economic policy. Second, white mainline Protestants loosened their GOP ties, with many defecting to Perot and Clinton. Although still within the Republican camp, mainliners are divided on both social and economic issues. Third, white Catholics returned to the Democratic fold, halting two decades of drift toward the GOP, but this reversal obscured serious rifts among Catholics over traditional values. Fourth, secular voters moved solidly into the Democratic coalition, where their consistent liberalism provided a sharp counterpoint to the across-the-board conservatism of evangelicals. Members of smaller religious traditions, including black Protestants and Jews, played an important role, but displayed remarkable continuity in their traditional Democratic attachments. For simplicity's sake, then, we will focus here on the largest traditions: evangelical and mainline Protestants, Catholics, and seculars. These groups not only constitute the overwhelming majority of voters, but were also those most subject to political change.

The 1992 election reshuffled traditional alliances and rivalries among religious traditions, already modified by emerging cultural disputes and by cross-pressures created by current economic problems. As in the past, voters with strong religious commitments often held most firmly to their religious tradition's long-term partisan attachments, while the less committed were more influenced by short-term forces. But there was a new wrinkle: the highly committed in all religious traditions were also more conservative on social issues, potentially linking them together in opposition to a similar combination of less committed and more liberal members. When superimposed on the widening gulf between evangelical Protestants and seculars, these trends suggest that a new kind of party alignment is emerging: a division between religious and nonreligious voters from all traditions, replacing the old ethnoreligious politics based on disputes between religious traditions (Green and Guth 1991).

In this context, evangelical Protestants play a special role: they are a fulcrum on which both present and future party alignments rest. Their key position in the GOP coalition comes at the end of thirty years of realignment and is now strong enough to persist even in a very bad Republican year. And the limits of their support for the party may not have been reached: there is still considerable "upside potential" for the number of evangelicals identifying with and voting for the GOP. In addition, their turnout is still rising toward the higher rates of mainline Protestants and Catholics. The partisan attachments of evangelicals are magnified by their large and, perhaps, growing numbers, bolstered by high religious commitment, and fostered by conviction that religion is relevant to politics. Their Republican proclivities are likely to be enhanced, at least in the short run, by further gains in social status. All told, future party historians may well label 1992 the "Year of the Evangelical."[1]

We support these conclusions with evidence from several sources. First, to provide some needed historical context, we examine the University of Michigan's National Election Studies (NES) for 1960 and 1988. Although NES religion measures before 1990 leave much to be desired, if used carefully they reveal the restructuring of party coalitions over the last generation. Second, we look at the National Survey of Religion and Politics conducted at the University of Akron during the spring of 1992 to establish a baseline on the eve of the campaign. This survey has the advantage of numerous highly detailed measures of religion. Third, we mine the Voter Research and Surveys (VRS) exit polls for data on election-day voters. While these surveys are marred by poor religious items, they offer valuable information on a massive sample of actual voters. Finally, we turn to the 1992 NES's improved battery of religious items for the post-election situation. To produce roughly comparable measures for all surveys, we employ two fairly simple variables: religious tradition (cf. Kellstedt and Green 1993) and church attendance, which will serve as a proxy for religious commitment (Wald *et al.* 1993). We should note, however, that more elaborate measures of religious affiliation, beliefs, and commitment, when available, produce even stronger results than those reported here.[2]

---

[1] George Gallup, Jr. first referred to 1976 as the "Year of the Evangelical," a phrase later adopted widely by both the religious and secular media (see Woodward 1976).

[2] For detailed examination of the relative influence of a variety of religious, ideological and socioeconomic measures on political behavior, consult Kellstedt (1993). For discussion of our religious tradition measure, see the Appendix.

RELIGIOUS TRADITIONS AND PARTY COALITIONS 1960-1988

Since at least the mid-nineteenth century, American party coalitions have been comprised of competing ethnoreligious alignments, based on rival world views, life-styles, and negative reference groups (cf. McCormick 1986; Swierenga 1990). First the Whigs, and then the Republicans, were primarily the party of culturally dominant Protestants, the forebears of today's mainline churches, while the Democrats were a collection of cultural minorities, including Catholics, Jews, secular "free-thinkers," and interestingly enough, many sectarian Protestants, the spiritual predecessors of today's evangelicals. The exact makeup of these coalitions varied considerably by locale and over time, but their basic contours were still visible in 1992. Social scientists and survey researchers, however, have been slow to recognize these cultural patterns (cf. Swierenga 1990: 145-49 on this point). Not until the most recent eruption of religious politics during the Reagan era did political analysts pay much attention to measuring religious variables accurately (Wald and Smidt 1993). In fact, their initial confusion over the role of evangelical voters in the 1980s resulted from the deficiencies of religious measures in most polls (cf. Bruce 1988:95-103). Our analysis here has benefitted from recent advances in this area (Kellstedt 1993).

Present-day party alignments result from a reshuffling of historic patterns since 1960, changes illustrated by data from the 1960 and 1988 National Election Studies, shown in Table 1 (cf. Kellstedt et al. 1991). Perhaps the most significant shift from the old alignments involved evangelical Protestants: in 1960, fully 60 percent identified as Democrats, but by 1988 only 40 percent did, while Republican affiliation rose from only 32 percent to 48 percent among all evangelicals. The reaction to Roman Catholic John Kennedy's candidacy in 1960 foretold the trajectory of evangelical presidential voting, which by 1988 was decisively Republican. By the late 1980s, this Republicanism extended to offices down the ballot, such as the House of Representatives. In 1960, for example, while endorsing Nixon by a large margin, evangelicals gave only 41 percent of their votes to Republican House candidates; by 1988 this proportion was 52 percent. Note that all these shifts were magnified for regular church attenders, those most deeply engaged in their faith and thus most receptive to religious cues. Of equal importance is the evangelical community's size: despite the massive social transformations of this era, they remained at one-quarter of the adult population, with regular attenders actually increasing slightly in "market share."

TABLE 1

Religious Tradition, Church Attendance and Political Behavior, 1960 and 1980*

Religious Tradition & Church Attendance	Party ID Dem	Party ID Rep	GOP Pres Vote	GOP House Vote	Vote Turn Out	% Pop
Evangelical Protestant						
1960 All	60	32	60	41	72	26
Regular Attenders	55	38	77	52	80	10
1988 All	40	48	70	52	64	26
Regular Attenders	36	53	72	63	77	12
Mainline Protestant						
1960 All	37	54	69	63	86	41
Regular Attenders	36	58	75	63	91	15
1988 All	36	55	65	51	79	27
Regular Attenders	33	62	69	56	92	8
Roman Catholic						
1960 All	73	19	18	19	89	20
Regular Attenders	77	13	14	18	93	15
1988 All	50	40	54	39	78	24
Regular Attenders	57	38	49	39	90	10
Secular						
1960 All	40	30	46	55	55	8
1988 All	41	37	41	37	62	9

Source: National Election Studies, University of Michigan, 1960 and 1988.
*All numbers in percent. See Appendix for further information.

The evangelical realignment was not, however, a steady process. The defini-tive movement was quite abrupt, occurring during the 1984 Reagan landslide. The Nixon triumph in 1972 had produced an earlier high point of Republican voting (but not GOP identification), but the candidacies of Southern Baptist Jimmy Carter in 1976 and 1980 slowed the Republican trend. Thus, when ana-lysts looked at "born again" voters, they variously concluded that evangelicals were tending Republican, were still largely Democratic, or were sharply divided (cf. Himmelstein 1990:109-28). With the benefit of hindsight, the pattern is much clearer: the changes rumored among evangelicals in the 1970s and 1980s were indeed underway, but not yet fully realized (Smidt 1993). Changes in iden-tification and behavior among a voting bloc of this magnitude obviously had enormous ramifications for American politics (Dionne 1991:209-41).

The evangelical conversion finally united the two white Protestant traditions in the GOP. By 1988 evangelicals nearly matched mainline Protestants in Republican affiliation, and actually voted Republican more often in presidential and congressional elections. The political behavior of mainliners changed little over the period, but their numbers declined dramatically, decreasing by more than one-third overall and by nearly one-half in regular church attenders. Thus, by 1988 evangelical and mainline voting blocs were of equal size, but church-going evangelicals greatly outnumbered their mainline counterparts. Mainliners sustained their historic prominence in the GOP coalition by a decreasing margin, largely on the basis of greater turnout (Kellstedt et al. 1991).

During this period Catholics were also on the move. Overwhelmingly Democratic in 1960, they shifted toward the GOP in both affiliation and voting at the presidential and congressional levels, but remained marginally Democratic in 1988. But unlike the situation among evangelicals, observant Catholics did not lead the exodus toward the Republicans. While some Catholic traditionalists, especially among younger voters, turned to the GOP on cultural and foreign policy issues (accounting for many "Reagan Democrats"), others remained loyal to their ancestral party; a similar division occurred among less committed Catholics (Kenski and Lockwood 1991). Over the period, Catholics gained in number, at least matching each of the Protestant traditions, but regular attenders declined by one-third, to a number roughly equal to that of church-going evangelicals. Catholic turnout rates closely paralleled those of the Protestant mainline.

Although Republicans benefitted from such trends among evangelicals and Catholics, the Democrats increasingly depended on other traditions. Secular voters drifted toward the Democrats in presidential and congressional voting, and remained modestly Democratic in party identification, but their turnout lagged behind the other three major religious traditions (Erickson et al. 1989). According to the NES, they also became slightly more numerous. (We will see below, however, that precise measures of religious affiliation suggest much faster growth of secular voters.) The Democratic coalition was rounded out by two smaller traditions, black Protestant and Jewish voters. The former grew in size, Democratic affiliation, and turnout over the period (Wilcox 1991), while the latter declined in number, but remained solidly Democratic with high voting rates (Sigelman 1991).

What caused these shifts in party coalitions after 1960? At the risk of oversimplification, there were two important factors: social issue polarization and upward social mobility (Green and Guth 1993). Over this period, a powerful new divide opened on social issues, with defenders of traditional values and social arrangements fighting advocates of cosmopolitan values and new lifestyles. In many respects, foreign policy disputes paralleled this cultural divide. At the same time, however, the country experienced dramatic gains in socioeconomic status, with some historically disadvantaged groups, such as evangelicals and Catholics, gaining the most in relative terms. For evangelicals, these trends interacted to generate support for the GOP, the more conservative party on both counts, although cultural polarization clearly mattered most. These same trends cross-pressured mainline Protestants and Catholics, moving some toward the

GOP and others toward the Democrats. Secular voters faced a similar situation, but as social issues such as abortion and gay rights became increasingly important more of them moved in a Democratic direction. Contemporary social movements surely played a role in fostering these new alignments, including the Christian Right and the pro-life movement on the one hand, and feminist, gay, and civil rights movements on the other, but the precise magnitude of their impact on the scope, form, and pace of these changes is far from clear (Wilcox 1992; Wuthnow 1989).

Thus, the ethnoreligious structure of party coalitions at the ascension of George Bush in 1989 was a variant of the historical pattern: the GOP was the party of (united) Protestantism, leavened with conservatives from other religious backgrounds, while the Democrats remained the party of cultural minorities, with increased numbers of secular voters, black Protestants, and a smattering of liberals from other traditions. During the 1980s, this alignment favored Republicans at the presidential level and Democrats at the congressional, but there were great tensions in both coalitions (Shafer 1991). First Ronald Reagan and then George Bush cemented their coalition with a careful mix of social, economic and foreign policy conservatism; congressional Democrats attracted votes with a skillfully wrapped package of tangible and symbolic benefits.

THE SPRING OF 1992

Much had changed by the spring of 1992. The end of the Persian Gulf and Cold Wars robbed Republicans of key issues, a weak economy undermined Bush's popularity, and a primary challenge from Pat Buchanan damaged his credibility. The Democrats did not go unscathed, however, with scandals in Congress, accusations of gridlock, and the usual infighting in the Democratic primaries. Party alignments that seemed so solid four years before appeared to many observers to be in flux.

In Table 2 we present a snapshot of the ethnoreligious composition of party coalitions prior to the fall campaign using data from the National Survey of Religion and Politics conducted at the University of Akron in the spring of 1992. This picture suggests continuity with 1988, rather than change. Although this portrait is based on more sophisticated measures of religious tradition and behavior than available in the 1988 NES, the political patterns in Table 2 are strikingly similar to those in Table 1. The GOP allegiance of evangelicals had not wavered under Bush, and the relative positions of Catholics and secular voters remained static. All groups actually recalled more support for Bush in 1988 than Table 1 shows, and in addition, reported higher support for GOP House candidates in 1990. Only mainline Protestants experienced a modest decline in Republican allegiance, but this may reflect better measurement of religious affiliation in the Akron study, with some erroneously classified "mainline" (and staunchly Republican) voters in previous analysis being moved to the evangelical tradition. Note that mainline Protestants, particularly regular church attenders, are markedly less numerous in Table 2 than in Table 1, while seculars are nearly twice as common. The reason is straightforward: the Akron study data in Table 2 come from questions that minimize the social desirability effects of hav-

ing a religious preference, encouraging people with no religious affiliation to report just that (Kellstedt and Green 1993).

TABLE 2

Religious Tradition, Church Attendance and Political Behavior, Spring 1992*

Religious Tradition & Church Attendance	Party ID		1988 Bush Vote	1990 GOP Cong Vote	High Bush Eval	Plan Vote Bush 1992	% Pop
	Dem	Rep					
Evangelical Protestant							
All	34	48	72	57	43	54	25
Regular Attenders	30	55	75	62	44	60	13
Mainline Protestant							
All	32	51	67	58	38	51	20
Regular Attenders	31	54	70	57	42	56	6
Roman Catholic							
All	41	40	63	43	35	43	24
Regular Attenders	46	38	65	44	35	43	12
Secular							
All	41	34	53	46	28	37	16

Source: National Survey of Religion and Politics, University of Akron, 1992.
*All numbers in percent. See Appendix for further information.

Despite the basic continuity in alignments from 1988, Bush obviously faced
some serious political problems in spring 1992. As Table 2 shows, evaluations of
his presidency were quite low, with far less than 50 percent in each group giving
him "excellent" or "good" ratings. Worse yet, a much lower proportion of each
group planned to vote for him in 1992 than reported voting for him in 1988.
Still, evangelicals gave Bush the strongest support, followed in order by mainliners, Catholics, and seculars. And there were clear issue bases for this pattern.
Table 3 demonstrates that evangelicals were the most conservative on abortion,
gay and women's rights, with regular church attenders markedly more so. Mainliners and Catholics were less conservative, although regular attenders often
leaned more to the right, especially on abortion and among Catholics. Seculars
were by far the most liberal on social issues. These data suggest that the social
issue conservatism linked to religious beliefs, religious traditions, and involvement clearly structured partisan and electoral choices. Indeed, the contrast between the more and less committed people in each tradition, as well as the sharp
split between evangelicals and seculars, helps account for persistent rumors of a
"culture war" in American politics (Hunter 1991).

TABLE 3

Religious Tradition, Church Attendance and Issue Position, Spring 1992*

Religious Tradition & Church Attendance	Pro Choice	Pro Women Rights	Pro Gay Rights	Gov Aid Black Rights	Gov Health Insur.	Pro Envir.	Back Israel	Cut Defense
Evangelical Protestant								
All	46	52	35	35	55	56	42	45
Regular Attenders	29	45	26	34	49	54	48	43
Mainline Protestant								
All	72	59	57	40	59	63	26	47
Regular Attenders	59	55	52	45	61	63	29	51
Roman Catholic								
All	60	61	59	39	63	58	22	51
Regular Attenders	44	57	57	41	63	58	23	52
Secular								
All	86	60	62	36	63	65	21	58

Source: National Survey of Religion and Politics, University of Akron, 1992.
*All numbers in percent. See Appendix for further information.

Evangelicals were not only social conservatives, but more surprisingly, were also the most conservative group on economic and domestic issues, including aid to minorities, national health insurance, and environmental regulation, if only by small margins. Once again, regular church attenders were even more conservative. As on social issues, mainliners and Catholics were more liberal than evangelicals on these domestic issues, but here their regular attenders were modestly more liberal. And with the exception of aid to minorities, seculars resembled the Protestant mainline. This pattern of opinion on domestic issues had many sources: growing ideological consistency among both evangelicals and seculars; the upward mobility of religious groups, with evangelicals gaining middle class status and seculars flooding into the "new class" professions; and selective perception on the part of committed partisans, including Republican evangelicals and Democratic seculars. As one might imagine, foreign policy concerns were of little importance in early 1992, but support for Israel and cutting defense spending were emblematic of the past power of these issues: evangelicals were the most pro-Israeli and pro-defense, and seculars at the other extreme on both (Guth and Fraser 1993).

So, on the eve of the 1992 general election campaign, Bush faced serious difficulties: eroding support for his presidency across the board, but particularly among mainline Protestants, a key constituency in 1988, with parallel declines among Catholics, a swing vote four years earlier, and among seculars, who had backed Michael Dukakis. Looked at another way, evangelicals were Bush's strongest supporters, holding conservative positions on both social and economic issues. Furthermore, social issues offered access to pockets of traditionalists among other groups. Given his problems with the economy, it is easy to see why Bush chose to make social issue appeals a major part of his campaign. By the same token, these data also reveal the basis for Pat Buchanan's primary challenge from the right, and for Bill Clinton's "New Covenant" platform during the general election, combining social issue moderation with domestic policy initiatives.

ELECTION DAY 1992

How did the 1992 campaign affect ethnoreligious elements in party coalitions? Our first evidence on this point comes from the widely quoted network exit polls from Voter Research and Surveys (VRS), reported in Tables 4 and 5. Unfortunately, VRS used very simplistic (and idiosyncratic) religious measures, and thus the results are not strictly comparable to other studies. As a religious tradition measure, VRS allowed voters the choices of "Protestant, Catholic, Other Christian, Jewish, Something Else, None." This permits no easy classification of evangelical and mainline Protestants, but fortunately, VRS also asked voters to check a box labeled "born-again Christian/Fundamentalist," if those terms applied. We used responses to this question in combination with the earlier one to produce evangelical and mainline categories. Of course, not all voters in the evangelical tradition respond positively to both "born-again" and "fundamentalist." Therefore, this operation produces fewer evangelicals and more mainline Protestants than the more accurate data reported in Tables 2 and 6, even after accounting for differences in turnout. Still, the patterns we find are consistent with more sophisticated pre- and post-election surveys.

On election day, according to VRS, evangelicals were Bush's strongest supporters: 63 percent of all evangelicals and 70 percent of regular church-goers among them voted for the president, a very impressive showing for a three-way race. Considering only the two-party vote, the analogous figures were 74 percent and 79 percent, respectively, higher than in 1988. Overall, evangelicals provided more than one-quarter of Bush's 1992 vote and regular attending evangelicals were roughly as important to Bush as black Protestants were to Clinton. In addition, evangelicals' GOP identification increased modestly from the spring, and they voted for Republican House candidates at *higher* rates than in 1988 and 1990. Southern Baptists Bill Clinton and Al Gore actually received a lower percentage of evangelical votes than Michael Dukakis did in 1988, despite midcampaign press reports of possible inroads among conservative Protestants.

TABLE 4

Religious Tradition, Church Attendance and Political Behavior, Election Day 1992*

Religious Tradition & Church Attendance	Party ID		Pres Vote		GOP House Vote	% Pop
	Dem	Rep	Dem	Rep		
Evangelical Protestant						
All	24	56	22	63	67	15
Regular Attenders	21	58	18	70	73	11
Mainline Protestant						
All	33	44	38	37	51	32
Regular Attenders	31	49	33	46	56	11
Roman Catholic						
All	42	34	41	36	46	22
Regular Attenders	44	33	39	41	47	10
Secular						
All	65	14	71	17	22	16

Source: General Election Exit Poll, Voter Research and Surveys, 1992.
*All numbers in percent. See Appendix for further information.

A much different result appeared among mainline Protestants, where Bush garnered less than two-fifths of the vote, and less than one-half even among regular church attenders. These figures paralleled declines in Republican identification and support for GOP congressional candidates. As we might expect, Catholics were even less supportive of Bush, although their behavior and party identification were not dramatically off the mark from previous elections. But a major shift did occur among secular voters: Bush received less than half the level of support that he enjoyed in 1988, while their party identification and congressional vote went solidly Democratic. By adding the customary huge Democratic majorities among black Protestants and Jews to his column, Clinton assembled a facsimile of the old New Deal religious coalition, but with some mainline Protestants and a growing corps of seculars replacing the departed evangelicals.

Ross Perot also absorbed some evangelicals dissatisfied with Bush who might have voted for Clinton. Overall, Perot received 15 percent from evangelicals, markedly less than from mainliners (25 percent) and Catholics (23 percent), but more than from seculars (12 percent). Clinton was the second choice among all groups of Perot voters, but least so among evangelicals (51 percent), followed by Catholics (58 percent), mainliners (61 percent) and seculars (78 percent). Perot supporters may have been a cross-section of the electorate in some respects, but not in religious tradition, or more significantly, religious commitment: in all traditions Perot voters attended church less regularly and were less involved religiously by almost any measure. This lack of religious commitment parallels their detachment from parties and other political institutions.

The VRS data also underscore the issue basis of the 1992 vote, presented in Table 5. The economy was clearly the most powerful issue and hurt Bush everywhere. Never more than one-third of any group gave the president "excellent" or "good" job ratings, markedly lower than in the spring, and a plurality in most groups claimed their personal financial situation had worsened since 1988. But as before, evangelicals consistently gave Bush the highest marks on the economy, significantly ahead of other traditions, and were also far less pessimistic about the future of the economy. An even starker contrast appears on the social issues: evangelicals were strongly pro-life and seculars as adamantly pro-choice, with mainline Protestants and Catholics falling in between. As before, regular attenders in all traditions were more pro-life than their co-religionists.

TABLE 5

Religious Tradition, Church Attendance and Issue Positions, Election Day 1992*

Religious Tradition & Church Attendance	Financial Situation Compared to 4 Yrs. Ago: Better	Worse	Pro Choice	State of Economy	Most Important Issues in Vote Decision Abortion/ Family Values	Deficit Econ Jobs	Other Domes Issues
Evangelical Protestant							
All	33	24	29	33	53	50	26
Regular Attenders	34	20	22	33	57	45	23
Mainline Protestant							
All	25	32	72	24	24	65	39
Regular Attenders	30	38	63	24	31	57	37
Roman Catholic							
All	23	36	62	19	22	66	39
Regular Attenders	22	35	47	19	27	63	39
Secular							
All	24	38	78	11	22	66	50

Source: General Election Exit Poll, Voter Research and Surveys, 1992.
*All numbers in percent. See Appendix for further information.

Similar patterns emerge for the issues that voters claim influenced their choice, revealing starkly different priorities across religious traditions. More than half the evangelicals identified abortion or family values as important, often twice the percentage of other groups. Indeed, social issue mentions decline from evangelicals to seculars, with the now familiar variations among regular church attenders. Something of an opposite pattern appears for those who mentioned the economy. Although evangelicals were concerned with these issues as well (50 percent mentions), the other traditions showed substantially more interest (average 66 percent mentions). Nonevangelicals also cited much greater concern for domestic issues such as health care, education and environmental regulation: only one-quarter of evangelicals mentioned these, compared to nearly one-half of seculars. These priorities clearly influenced votes: nearly 90 percent of regular attending evangelicals who named abortion as important voted for Bush, whereas 75 percent of seculars who named the economy as important voted for Clinton or Perot (data not shown).

Contrary to conventional wisdom, this evidence suggests that Bush's social issue appeals did *not* cost him the election. In fact, on balance social issues helped him. Among voters who supported Bush in both 1988 and 1992, just over two-fifths mentioned social issues as important to their vote, and an equal number named the economy. But of those who abandoned Bush for Clinton in 1992, only one-fifth mentioned social issues compared to almost three-quarters naming the economy. The numbers were even more lopsided for Bush voters who defected to Perot: about one-sixth mentioned social issues and more than four-fifths named the economy. All told, *the economy cost Bush more than four times as much support as social issues* (17 to 4 percent) among those who defected to Clinton or Perot. As one might imagine, these patterns were much stronger for evangelicals than for voters in the other traditions.

Clearly then, Bush held evangelicals and some other religious conservatives largely because of their views on social issues, aided by their less critical evaluation of the economy, while Clinton and Perot cashed in on economic discontent and domestic policy concerns among voters for whom social issues were less salient. Clinton's masterful focus on the economy, combined with Perot's erratic populism, effectively exploited the weaknesses in key Republican constituencies evident in the spring of 1992, expanding the Democrats' base of cultural minorities enough to win a three-way race. By the same token, Bush secured his base of cultural conservatives, but failed to assuage the economic worries of his key constituencies. Although social issue and economic appeals operated largely independently of one another, considerable polarization occurred between each party's core constituencies.

THE FALL OF 1992

Did these exit poll patterns persist after election day? The 1992 NES data allow us to confirm these findings and investigate further, with the help of more sophisticated measures of religion than are available in the VRS data (for further discussion of the new NES religion measures, see Leege and Kellstedt 1993). As Table 6 confirms, Bush held evangelicals to a remarkable degree, lost ground among mainliners and Catholics, and was soundly beaten among seculars. Overall, the 1992 NES results are strikingly similar to the comparable pre-election data from the Akron study (compare Table 6 to Table 2), but reveal some important, if subtle, effects from the campaign.

TABLE 6

Religious Tradition, Church Attendance and Political Behavior, Fall 1992*

Religious Tradition & Church Attendance	Party ID Dem	Party ID Rep	Pres Vote Dem	Pres Vote Rep	GOP HR Vote	Vote Turn Out	% Pop
Evangelical Protestant							
All	38	51	28	56	53	76	25
Regular Attenders	31	61	22	70	61	81	14
Mainline Protestant							
All	34	53	38	37	49	84	21
Regular Attenders	31	63	35	42	59	91	7
Roman Catholic							
All	51	38	45	31	42	86	24
Regular Attenders	43	44	41	36	44	88	11
Secular							
All	50	32	55	20	35	65	15

Source: National Election Studies, University of Michigan, 1992.
*All numbers in percent. See Appendix for further information.

After the election, evangelicals still identified Republican, *but in even larger numbers* than in the spring. Furthermore, their turnout far exceeded that in 1988 — but did not quite equal that of mainline Protestants and Catholics. Unlike the election-day VRS surveys, which showed mainliners far behind evangelicals in Republican identification, the NES survey has mainliners matching evangelicals in that respect. The NES agrees with VRS, however, in finding much greater voting support for Bush and GOP congressional candidates among evangelicals. As in the VRS survey, Catholics and seculars in the NES identified more often as Democrats and supported Democratic candidates at a higher rate than did either Protestant tradition, although the NES shows Catholic churchgoers to be significantly more Republican in identification and behavior than nonattenders. As in the VRS surveys, seculars identify and vote heavily Democratic, but their turnout rate still lagged behind the other traditions.

The issue basis of these post-election patterns seemed little changed from the spring. Table 7 provides information that parallels Table 3. Although the topics are the same, question wording and format in the Akron study and the NES differ enough to make direct comparisons problematic. The relative differences among religious traditions were clearly maintained, however, and perhaps even extended. As before, evangelicals (especially regular attenders) were most conservative across the board, but particularly on social issues. Mainline Protestants and Catholics sustained their relative positions, with Catholics more liberal and regular attenders in both traditions slightly more conservative than their less observant counterparts. The only exception is on abortion, where Catholics as a group were less pro-choice than the mainline and regular church-goers even more conservative. Secular voters, on the other hand, were the most liberal on all issues, often by wide margins.

TABLE 7

Religious Tradition, Church Attendance and Issue Positions, Fall 1992*

Religious Tradition & Church Attendance	Pro Choice	Pro Women Rights	Pro Gay Rights	Gov Aid Black Rights	Gov Health Insur.	Pro Envir.	Cut Defense
Evangelical Protestant							
All	42	64	44	13	41	53	31
Regular Attenders	25	52	32	12	34	43	29
Mainline Protestant							
All	77	75	59	17	42	56	50
Regular Attenders	66	73	53	15	38	48	44
Roman Catholic							
All	59	83	67	19	55	61	51
Regular Attenders	40	81	69	15	52	57	44
Secular							
All	83	85	69	26	61	70	53

Source: National Election Studies, University of Michigan, 1992.
*All numbers in percent. See Appendix for further information.

All these data reveal considerable polarization along partisan and cultural lines, with a gulf widening between evangelicals and seculars. But this development was temporarily obscured by the salience of economic issues among mainline Protestants, Catholics, and especially seculars. In fact, the 1992 election did not represent a rejection of social issue conservatism — any more than Reagan's election in 1980 represented an endorsement. Both elections largely turned on the economic failures of incumbent presidents. Even powerful economic concerns were filtered, however, through the ethnoreligious structure of the party coalitions. In 1980, both social and economic issues reinforced each other for evangelicals, while other groups responded to one or the other. But in 1992, social and economic issues moved in opposite directions, sweeping away part of the GOP's mainline and Catholic "economic" constituencies and revealing the cultural backbone of the party, much as Carter's defeat in 1980 lay bare the Democrats' core constituencies.

These patterns show the limitations of defining electoral alignments only in terms of short-term economic forces or even of long-term economic status. Evangelical and high-commitment mainline Protestants were generally less affluent and objectively most affected by the recession, and yet they stood most firmly behind Bush and the Republicans. Meanwhile, Jewish, secular and low-commitment mainline Protestant voters were generally more affluent and least burdened by hard times; yet they backed Clinton in large numbers. Perot voters were the most disconnected from both American political and religious life, and thus "available" for mobilization on the basis of economic discontent. All this reminds us that economic forces work *within* the cultural context.

Thus, the principal effect of 1992 was to bind evangelicals to the Republican party, much as black Protestants were cemented to the Democratic coalition in the 1960s. A secondary result was the acceleration of secular voters' migration toward the Democrats, much as evangelicals were pushed toward the GOP in 1984. And a third impact was the loosened Republicanism of mainline Protestants, paralleling the weakened Democratic attachments of Catholics from the last two decades. The changes and continuities among ethnoreligious groups make several scenarios possible. The GOP may try to resurrect the Reagan coalition by recovering attractive economic policies to parallel social issue conservatism, but it may be equally possible for Clinton to bolster a traditional Democratic coalition by delivering economic growth. Ironically, as president, Clinton must highlight liberal social policies to hold the seculars, much as Bush catered to religious conservatives, but the core cultural constituency of the Democratic party may not be enough to sustain Clinton's legislative program (Cook 1993). Whatever the outcome, many of these developments also point to the emergence of a new kind of party alignment.

A NEW KIND OF COALITION?

Ethnoreligious coalitions have always been messy affairs, fraught with internal tensions often incapable of any final resolution. The management of these tensions, however, sometimes points toward new and more consistent — if not always more productive — party alignments. Just as political controversy over the New Deal's pragmatic experimentalism resulted by 1964 in ideologically consistent parties, one liberal on economic management and the other conservative, the present ethnoreligious alliances point toward a new divide based on the extent rather than type of religious belief. Although elements of the older alignment will persist, increasingly the party coalitions may include, on one side, believers who organize their lives around religious commitments, while the other side would attract nonbelievers and those for whom religion is unimportant (Green and Guth 1991).

Such a cleavage would be new in American history, but has been quite common in European democracies, where socialist parties have often been adamantly secular, and conservative parties have frequently defended religious establishments (Berger 1982). While many factors have made American religion particularly vigorous, over the last thirty years secularizing processes have generated growing opposition to the influence of religion. The growth in the secular population has been mostly at the expense of more accommodated churches, particularly mainline Protestants and, ironically, has had the least effect on sectarian bodies, including evangelicals, who seem to prosper in opposition to secularizing forces. The developing conflict between evangelicals and seculars has been paralleled by battles between "modernists" and "traditionalists" within mainline and Catholic churches (Wuthnow 1988), and new alliances have been given form by various "ecumenical" and "nondenominational" movements that span even ancient religious boundaries (Jorstad 1990). The net result is to reconfigure religious traditions, the stuff of party coalitions, along broader and less particularistic lines.

Although this new alignment has not fully emerged, it is prefigured by the underlying cultural polarization in 1992, both between evangelicals and seculars, and between the more and less committed members of the major religious traditions. This cleavage is already well-advanced among cultural elites (Hunter 1991), religious professionals (Guth et al. 1991), party contributors (Green et al. 1991), and interest group activists (Green and Guth 1990). And, whether intentionally or not, antagonists on both sides of the cultural chasm are digging it deeper. On the religious side, Christian Right groups such as the Christian Coalition, Concerned Women of America, and Focus on the Family are amassing impressive resources to mobilize evangelical voters. Although they have not yet overcome historic animosities within their own tradition, they can help solidify one element of a broader traditionalist coalition in the GOP. Organizations such as People For the American Way and the American Civil Liberties Union may have similar effects for the secular and less religious groups in the Democratic party.

At this juncture, the Christian Right has far more raw political resources than the "secular left," but the latter campaigns with media and educational elites on its side. Intense conflict over cultural issues could well push elements of other traditions toward such an alignment, but for the new divide to become dominant, it must reach beyond cultural questions to include economic matters as well. In 1992 only among evangelicals and seculars did we observe consistent conservatism and liberalism on both kinds of issues, and some evangelical activists, at least, believe that such a broader agenda is necessary and possible (Seib 1993). Given their new-found political unity and their strong institutional base, evangelicals are the logical place to look for expansion of the "culture war" to other fronts.

Thus, the dominant interpretive theme of 1992, "It's the economy, stupid" (attributed to Clinton adviser James Carville), fails to capture the full significance of that contest. What we see is the first rumblings of an electoral culture war. In one sense, 1992 may be remembered as the "Year of the Evangelical," in which activists mounted impressive grassroots campaigns among an Evangelical public more receptive than ever. It is safe to predict that this mobilization will continue or even intensify in future local, state, and national elections. By the same token, however, 1992 could be characterized as the "Year of the Secular," reflecting the growing importance of this often-underestimated bloc of predominantly liberal voters. The new role of evangelicals and seculars as the cultural cores of the Republican and Democratic parties, respectively, puts them in key positions to shape the ideological contours of those parties. Ironically, mainline Protestants and Catholics, long the centerpieces of the Republican and Democratic party coalitions, are now "swing" constituencies, in many instances most responsive to short-term economic conditions.

The 1992 election indeed resulted in significant changes in the religious traditions that have been the backbone of party coalitions for most of American history. At present such alignments still structure party politics and are quite potent even when economic issues come to the fore. They are likely to be even more important during times of peace and prosperity, perhaps evolving into a more comprehensive religious alignment. For good or ill, observers cannot afford to ignore the role of religion in politics.

REFERENCES

Berger, S. (ed.). 1982. *Religion in West European Politics*. London: Cass.

Bruce, S. 1988. *The Rise and Fall of the New Christian Right*. Oxford: Oxford University Press.

Cook, R. 1993. "Clinton struggles to meld a governing coalition." *Congressional Quarterly Weekly Report* 51:2175-79.

Dionne, E. J. 1991. *Why Americans Hate Politics*. New York: Simon and Schuster.

Erickson, R. S., T. D. Lancaster, and D. W. Romero. 1989. "Group components of the presidential vote, 1952-1984." *Journal of Politics* 51:337-45.

Green, J. C. and J. L. Guth. 1990. "Politics in a new key." *Western Political Quarterly* 43:153-79.

_____. 1991. "The Bible and the ballot box," pp. 207-26 in Guth and Green, *q.v.*

_____. 1993. "From lambs to sheep," pp. 100-17 in Leege and Kellstedt, *q.v.*

_____ and C. R. Fraser. 1991. "Religion and politics among party activists," pp. 113-36 in Guth and Green, *q.v.*

Guth, J. L. and J. C. Green (eds.). 1991. *The Bible and the Ballot Box*. Boulder, CO: Westview.

Guth, J. L, J. C. Green, L. A. Kellstedt, and C. E. Smidt. 1993. "God's own party." *Christian Century* (Feb.):172-76.

Guth, J. L., J. C. Green, C. E. Smidt, and M. M. Poloma. 1991. "Pulpits and politics," pp. 73-93 in Guth and Green, *q.v.*

Guth, J. L. and C. R. Fraser. 1993. "Religion and foreign policy attitudes." Paper presented at the annual meeting of the American Political Science Association, Washington, DC.

Himmelstein, J. L. 1990. *To the Right*. Berkeley: University of California Press.

Hunter, J. D. 1991. *Culture Wars*. New York: Basic Books.

Jorstad, E. 1990. *Holding Fast/Pressing On*. New York: Praeger.

Keith, B., D. B. Magleby, C. J. Nelson, E. Orr, M. C. Westlye, and R. E. Wolfinger. 1992. *The Myth of the Independent Voter*. Berkeley: University of California Press.

Kellstedt, L. A. 1993. "Religion, the neglected variable," pp. 273-303 in Leege and Kellstedt, *q.v.*

Kellstedt, L. A. and J. C. Green. 1993. "Knowing God's many people," pp. 53-71 in Leege and Kellstedt, *q.v.*

Kellstedt, L. A., C. E. Smidt, and P. M. Kellstedt. 1991. "Religious tradition, denomination, and commitment," pp. 139-58 in Guth and Green, *q.v.*

Kenski, H. C. and W. Lockwood. 1991. "Catholic voting behavior in 1988," pp. 173-87 in Guth and Green, *q.v.*

Ladd, E. C. 1993. "The 1992 vote for President Clinton." *Political Science Quarterly* 108:1-28.

Leege, D. C. and L. A. Kellstedt (eds.). 1993. *Rediscovering the Religious Factor in American Politics*. Armonk, NY: Sharpe.

Lipset, S. M. 1993. "The significance of the 1992 election." *PS* 56:7-16.

McCormick, R. L. 1986. *Party, Period and Public Policy*. New York: Oxford University Press.

Nelson, M. (ed.). 1993. *The Elections of 1992*. Washington, DC: CQ Press.

Pomper, G. (ed.). 1993. *The Election of 1992*. Chatham, NJ: Chatham House.

Seib, G. F. 1993. "Christian coalition hopes to expand by taking stands on taxes, crime, health care and NAFTA." *Wall Street Journal* (Sept. 7): A16.

Shafer, B. (ed.). 1991. *The End of Realignment?* Madison: University of Wisconsin Press.

Sigelman, L. 1991. "Jews and the 1988 election," pp. 188-203 in Guth and Green, *q.v.*

Smidt, C. E. 1993. "Evangelical voting patterns," pp. 85-117 in M. Cromartie (ed.), *No Longer Exiles*. Washington, DC: Ethics and Public Policy Center.

Swierenga, R. P. 1990. "Ethnoreligious political behavior in the mid-nineteenth century," pp. 146-71 in M. A. Noll (ed.), *Religion & American Politics*. New York: Oxford University Press.

Wald, K. D., L. A. Kellstedt, and D. C. Leege. 1993. "Church involvement and political behavior," pp. 139-56 in Leege and Kellstedt, *q.v.*

Wald, K. D. and C. E. Smidt. 1993. "Measurement strategies in the study of religion and politics," pp. 26-49 in Leege and Kellstedt, *q.v.*

Wilcox, C. 1991. "Religion and electoral politics among black Americans," pp. 159-72 in Guth and Green, *q.v.*

_____. 1992. *God's Warriors*. Baltimore, MD: Johns Hopkins University Press.

Woodward, K. 1976. "Born-again." *Newsweek* (Oct. 25): 68-76.

Wuthnow, R. 1988. *The Restructuring of American Religion*. Princeton, NJ: Princeton University Press.

_____. 1989. *The Struggle for America's Soul*. Grand Rapids, MI: Eerdmans.

APPENDIX: VARIABLE CONSTRUCTION

Religious Tradition

The major difficulty in defining religious traditions is distinguishing between mainline and evangelical Protestants. Our classification is based on extended analysis of the history and beliefs of specific denominations. Briefly, mainline Protestants come from theologically moderate to liberal churches, such as the Episcopal Church, the United Church of Christ, the Presbyterian Church in the U.S.A., and the United Methodist Church, while Evangelicals identify with more theologically conservative bodies, including most Baptist, Pentecostal, and Holiness groups, along with many nondenominational churches, and a scattering of the smaller denominations from the Presbyterian, Lutheran, and Wesleyan families. Despite some similarities with both mainline and evangelical Protestants, black Protestants constitute a separate religious tradition, and because this tradition is often difficult to identify from survey data, our analysis here is of white voters only. Secular voters are those who have no denominational identification or, if they do, show no evidence of religious interest or involvement beyond that preference. For a more elaborate discussion of the criteria used in classification and a list of denominations, see Kellstedt (1993:300) and Kellstedt and Green (1993).

In Tables 1, 2, 3, 6 and 7 we follow this denominational scheme as closely as possible. The National Election Studies prior to 1990 present difficulties for Table 1 because of an outmoded denominational code, but the 1992 Akron and NES surveys in Tables 2, 3, 6, and 7 utilize the new classification system. The VRS exit polls (Tables 4 and 5) present special problems, as they do not ask for voters' denominational affiliation. Using questions available, we defined mainliners as Protestants and Other Christians who do not identify as "born again Christian/fundamentalists," and evangelicals as those who do so identify.

Church Attendance

Individuals who attend church once a week or more were classified as "regular attenders."

Political Variables

Tables 1, 2, 4, and 6 use standard NES party identification items, with independents who report feeling closer to one party treated as party identifiers (Keith *et al.* 1992). In Table 2, the Bush evaluation is a five-point Likert scale, and the combination of the two highest points is reported ("excellent" and "good"). The 1992 vote intention item asked about voting for Bush, his "Democratic opponent," or "other candidate."

The issue questions in Table 3 are five-point Likert scale items, with the exception of abortion, which was a four-point scale. In Table 5, the abortion item was a four-point scale, the respondent's own financial situation was a three-point scale, and the evaluation of the economy was a four-point scale (the combination of "excellent" and "good" is reported). The abortion item in Table 7 is identical to the four-point item in Table 3; although the other items in Table 7 parallel the topics in Table 3, their wording and format differ, including both five- and seven-point Likert scales. Additional information is available from the authors.

7

Pat Robertson and the GOP: 1988 and Beyond*

James M. Penning
Calvin College

     This chapter examines the impact of Pat Robertson on the GOP, focusing on both the 1988 Bush-Robertson split and on recent activities of Robertson's Christian Coalition. An examination of Bush and Robertson delegates to 1988 GOP conventions in three states reveals marked differences between the two groups with respect to demographic characteristics, issue positions, level of political activity, and partisan attachment. In general, Robertson delegates conformed more closely to the "amateur" model than did Bush delegates. Post-1988 activities of Robertson's Christian Coalition have continued to divide the GOP. Nevertheless, both the Clinton victory and a more tolerant attitude among Christian Coalition leadership may facilitate the development of future GOP unity. Despite the presence of serious intraparty factionalism, the GOP may benefit from the infusion of a new group of Christian Right activists.

For over a decade, Pat Robertson and the Christian Right have played an important role in Republican party politics. In part, this reflects the energy and commitment with which his supporters have entered the political arena. However, it also stems from the opportunity to take advantage of post-1968 reforms which "opened up" both Republican and Democratic party nominating processes, making primaries the dominant method of selecting delegates to state and national conventions. Proponents argued that the reforms were necessary to ensure more equitable representation in party governance. However, critics charged that this new openness would threaten party unity by encouraging an influx of political "amateurs" into party politics (Wilson 1962) — persons who would place principle above pragmatism, write party platforms detrimental to building majority coalitions, and seek the nomination of extremist candidates with little chance of electoral success (Ranney 1975; Kirkpatrick 1976).

    Robertson's 1988 presidential candidacy seemed to confirm the critics' fears. Both reporters (Barnes 1986; Church 1986; Phillips 1988) and scholars (Guth and Green 1987; Green and Guth 1988; Oldfield 1988) portrayed Robertson's

* The author wishes to acknowledge the assistance of the Ray C. Bliss Institute of Applied Politics, the University of Akron, John C. Green, Director, for financial aid in collecting the Michigan data; Douglas Hodgkin of Bates College in providing the Maine data; and Tod A. Baker, Robert P. Steed, and Laurence W. Moreland of The Citadel for supplying the South Carolina data. The author also wishes to thank Carolyn Murray of the Maine Republican Party for providing information about the 1988 Maine Republican convention.

supporters as political "amateurs" — newly-mobilized, ideologically-driven, and more committed to the candidate than to the party. In contrast, supporters of George Bush were portrayed as more likely to be "professionals" — long-time Republicans, pragmatic rather than ideological, and more committed to the party than to the candidate.

Although Robertson lost the GOP nomination to Bush, one might expect his supporters to have a continuing, important impact on the party. As Kessel (1988:116) points out, some newly-mobilized party activists remain in party politics despite the fact that their candidate may have lost. Because these newcomers must contend with party regulars mobilized during previous campaigns, the newly-mobilized activists never completely dominate the party. Nevertheless, the newcomers can make a difference; the party never reverts to its previous condition, as the new activists influence both the internal operations and external perceptions of the party (see Baker *et al.* 1991; Eldersveld 1964; Sorauf and Beck 1988).

This study examines the impact of Pat Robertson on the Republican party by focusing on two questions. First, how serious was the Bush-Robertson split in 1988? And second, what are the long-term implications of the Robertson phenomenon for the GOP? In order to answer these questions, this study first examines Robertson and Bush delegates to the 1988 Republican conventions in three states — Michigan, Maine, and South Carolina.[1] By comparing the two groups of delegates in terms of demographic characteristics, issue positions, level of political activity, and partisan attachment, we can better understand both the degree of intraparty fragmentation caused by Robertson and the potential value of the recruitment of new party activists. In addition, this study discusses the post-1988 political activity of Robertson supporters in an effort to assess the long-term partisan implications.

BUSH AND ROBERTSON DELEGATES: 1988

Focusing on Michigan, Maine, and South Carolina offers distinct advantages for examining the impact of Robertson on the GOP. First, these states provide exceedingly diverse socioeconomic and political contexts, enhancing the external validity of the findings. Equally important, in each state Robertson's forces were sufficiently strong to generate substantial conflict at the 1988 state Republican conventions. As a result, each state represents a potential location of serious, long-term division within the GOP.

The Bush-Robertson split in Michigan was unusually bitter. In August, 1986, Robertson forces, with help from the Virginia-based Freedom Council, shocked Bush supporters by winning approximately half of the delegates to that year's state GOP convention. Although Robertson's strong 1986 showing had few consequences for the selection of delegates to the national GOP convention

---

[1] An initial, previously published study (Smidt and Penning 1990) focused only on delegates to the 1988 Michigan Republican state convention.

two years later, it demonstrated the presence of deep divisions in the party, with both Bush and Robertson forces preparing for a divisive 1988 struggle.

Thus, it is not surprising that 1987-1988 produced severe political conflict within the Michigan GOP, with Bush and Robertson forces battling each other in the courts as well as at the polls. Supporters of the two candidates vied with each other and with supporters of Jack Kemp for control of county conventions that were to select delegates to the state convention scheduled for January, 1988, in Grand Rapids (Hertzke 1993:141). The conflict grew so severe and became so confusing that Bush aide, Richard Bond, labeled Michigan "the Beirut of Republican politics" (Dionne 1988). At least 26 of Michigan's counties produced competing conventions controlled by the various warring factions, with each voting to send its own slate of delegates to the state convention (Hornbeck and Petykiewicz 1988:A1). Although Robertson and Kemp delegates dominated the so-called "rump" or "breakaway" county conventions, Bush supporters dominated most of the official (and, ultimately, court-sanctioned) county conventions.

When the state convention gathered to select delegates to the national convention, hundreds of Robertson supporters stormed out of the convention hall and into the overcrowded basement where, cheering wildly, they formed a rump convention and were addressed by Pat Robertson himself. The rump convention allocated 43 delegates to Robertson, 21 to Jack Kemp, and 13 to George Bush. Meanwhile, the official state convention, meeting upstairs, allocated 37 delegates to Bush, 32 to Kemp, and only 8 to Robertson (Wilkerson *et al.* 1988). Hostility toward the Robertson "rebels" ran high as indicated by the Republican state chairman's observation that Robertson's supporters looked like "the bar scene out of Star Wars" (Hertzke 1989:6). Party leaders predicted that the wounds created by the Bush-Robertson conflict would take a long time to heal.

In contrast to Michigan, there was no formal split at the Maine Republican convention in 1988, possibly because the Robertson forces were not as numerous or well-organized as in Michigan. Even before the 1988 Maine Republican state convention, Robertson's support had started to fade, and party leaders had begun looking for ways to unify the party for the upcoming presidential election. Yet in Maine too the Robertson forces demonstrated considerable strength. Conflict between Bush and Robertson forces was apparent, and as in Michigan, the state GOP faced a difficult task of reconciling the Bush and Robertson forces after the 1988 convention.

In South Carolina, the intensity of the conflict between Bush and Robertson supporters equaled or perhaps even surpassed that in Michigan. Robertson campaign organizers targeted South Carolina early, believing that if he could not succeed there it was doubtful he could win elsewhere. In 1987, Robertson forces, largely newcomers to the party, organized themselves as the Carolina Conservative Coalition (CCC) and succeeded in ousting a number of long-time party regulars at the Republican precinct meetings. In particular, they succeeded in gaining control of the Charleston County Republican party, located in one of the state's three largest urban areas, and did well in Richland County, the site of the state capitol, Columbia (Baker *et al.* 1991:95-96).

The ousted regulars fought back (unsuccessfully) with legal action and appeals to the party apparatus. Since South Carolina Republicans were using a primary election to select national convention delegates, these maneuverings, taken at face value, made little sense. However, the national convention delegates were to be bound only on the first two ballots, and Robertson supporters anticipated a multiple-ballot nomination process. Nevertheless, Bush benefitted from the advice of campaign manager, Lee Atwater (a South Carolina native) and the endorsement of Governor Caroll Campbell. Bush delegates outnumbered Robertson delegates at the 1988 South Carolina Convention, and Bush easily won the 1988 South Carolina primary, winning 48.6 percent of the vote (compared with 20.7 percent for Dole and 19.2 percent for Robertson). This victory generated momentum for Bush which helped him succeed on "Super Tuesday," three days later, and ultimately to win the Republican nomination (Baker *et al.* 1991:95-96).

Demographic Characteristics

Data for this analysis were generated from questionnaires distributed to delegates attending the 1988 Michigan, Maine, and South Carolina Republican state conventions.[2] A previous analysis of these data (Penning 1992) revealed a few differences between the Bush and Robertson delegates in terms of gender or place of residence. However, Table 1 demonstrates that the two groups of delegates differed markedly in age, income, and education, with Bush supporters tending to be older, better-educated, and higher in income than Robertson supporters.

In view of Robertson's background as a minister and religious broadcaster, it is not surprising that marked religious differences were found between Bush and Robertson delegates. But the magnitude of those differences is indeed notable. Table 1 reveals that Robertson drew heavily on charismatic Christians for his delegate support, while Bush received almost no support from charismatics.[3] Robertson delegates were also far more likely than Bush delegates to classify themselves as evangelicals. Although Bush did slightly better among evangelicals than among charismatics, Robertson proved far more popular than Bush among both groups. Marked differences were also evident in frequency of church attendance, with Robertson delegates exhibiting much higher levels of religiosity.[4]

---

[2] Data collection methods varied somewhat by state. The Michigan data were drawn from mail questionnaires sent to a sample of delegates, while the Maine and South Carolina data were drawn from questionnaires distributed to all delegates at the state GOP conventions. The total number of delegate responses and response rates for each state were as follows: Michigan 927 (53 percent), Maine 614 (41 percent), and South Carolina 644 (65 percent). Party officials in Maine were unable to give precise figures concerning the total number of convention delegates. However, officials estimated that approximately 1,500 delegates attended the convention, producing an estimated response rate of 41 percent. (For additional information on sampling techniques, see Penning 1992.)

[3] Other studies (e.g., Wilcox 1991) also demonstrate Robertson's strong support among charismatic Christians.

[4] Similar differences between Bush and Robertson delegates were found at the 1988 Virginia state Republican convention (McGlennon 1989).

TABLE 1

Socioeconomic Characteristics of Bush and Robertson Supporters at 1988 State Republican Conventions

| | Michigan | | | Maine | | | South Carolina | | |
Characteristics:	Bush Supporters (%)	Robertson Supporters (%)	Measure of Association	Bush Supporters (%)	Robertson Supporters (%)	Measure of Association	Bush Supporters (%)	Robertson Supporters (%)	Measure of Association
Age									
18-40 years	26.5	43.5		26.6	58.6		23.9	57.5	
41-60 years	49.7	46.0	v = .22***	45.8	33.6	v = .31***	44.0	29.0	v = .35***
61 years or older	23.8	10.5		27.6	7.8		32.0	13.6	
Family Income									
Below $35,000	28.2	43.0		38.9	62.0		28.0	43.9	
$35,00-60,000	34.8	42.0	v = .25***	35.7	24.0	v = .20***	36.4	39.6	v = .22***
Over $60,000	37.0	15.1		25.4	14.0		35.6	16.6	
Education									
Some College or Less	41.0	55.7		38.1	53.5		39.0	44.4	
College Graduate	23.4	20.7	v = .16***	33.2	32.6	v = .17***	27.7	32.1	v = .11
Post-Graduate	35.6	23.6		28.7	14.0		33.3	23.5	
Religion									
Charismatic	2.7	57.3	phi = .60***	2.7	41.3	phi = .51***	6.3	60.9	phi = .59***
Noncharismatic	97.3	42.7		97.3	58.7		93.7	39.1	
Evangelical	12.3	59.6	phi = .49***	6.0	49.2	phi = .50***	12.3	50.0	phi = .41***
Nonevangelical	87.7	40.4		94.0	50.8		87.7	50.0	
Church Attendance									
Every week or more	36.8	89.4		28.6	81.0		55.0	95.3	
Almost weekly, 1-2 per month	32.3	8.7	v = .55***	30.8	11.9	v = .47***	31.0	4.2	v = .45***
Few times per year, never	30.8	1.9		40.7	7.1		14.0	.5	
(Minimum N)	(319)	(298)		(347)	(121)		(250)	(187)	

***Chi square statistically significant at .001 level

Issue Positions

Table 2 provides data on delegates' issue positions in three key areas — domestic "moral" issues, domestic economic issues, and foreign/defense issues.[5] In all three states, Bush and Robertson supporters differed markedly over moral issues, with Robertson delegates being far more likely to endorse traditional, conservative issue positions. The biggest gaps appeared concerning issues emphasized by Robertson in his campaign — abortion, school prayer, and Bible reading in public schools. Although Bush delegates in South Carolina tended to be more conservative on domestic moral issues than were Bush delegates in either Michigan or Maine, they still proved to be less conservative than Robertson delegates in any of the states.

Differences tended to be much smaller on economic issues. In all three states, both Bush and Robertson delegates overwhelmingly supported across-the-board cuts in spending to balance the federal budget. Bush and Robertson delegates also gave overwhelming support to environmental protection regulations, though support was stronger among Bush delegates, particularly in Michigan. Only small minorities of Bush and Robertson delegates in any state endorsed either across-the-board tax increases or public works programs.

Finally, Robertson delegates proved to be consistently more "pro-defense" than Bush delegates. Both groups tended to support the Strategic Defense Initiative (SDI), although Robertson delegates generally gave higher levels of support. Greater disagreement occurred over increased defense spending and increased United States military presence in the Middle East and Latin America, with Robertson delegates tending to be more "pro-defense." The largest difference concerned the INF treaty; while large majorities of Bush delegates endorsed the treaty, fewer than half of Robertson delegates did so.

Thus, we see that issue cleavages over moral and foreign/defense issues tended to be substantial, while cleavages over economic issues were smaller. Apparently, then, economic issues provided the primary linkage between the "Christian Right" supporters of Robertson and the more traditional party regulars supporting Bush.

Nevertheless, one must view these issue differences within a broader context. Divisions may not be as great as they first appear in that the issue positions of Bush supporters may be closer to those of Robertson supporters than they are to those of Democratic party activists. Table 3 permits us to compare the responses of delegates to the 1988 Maine and South Carolina Republican conventions with those of delegates to their respective state Democratic conventions. The table reveals that with respect to nine of the thirteen policy

---

[5] An examination of the self-classified political ideology of Bush and Robertson delegates revealed that over eighty percent of both Bush and Robertson delegates in each state classified themselves as political conservatives. However, Robertson delegates tended to place themselves further to the right; while over thirty percent of the Robertson delegates in each state classified themselves as "extremely conservative," fewer than twenty percent of the Bush delegates did so. (For a complete summary of the ideological differences between the two groups of delegates, see Penning 1992.)

TABLE 2

Issue Positions of Bush and Robertson Supporters at 1988 State Republican Conventions

Characteristics:	Michigan			Maine			South Carolina		
	Bush Supporters (%)	Robertson Supporters (%)	Measure of Association	Bush Supporters (%)	Robertson Supporters (%)	Measure of Association	Bush Supporters (%)	Robertson Supporters (%)	Measure of Association
Domestic "Moral" Issues									
Equal Rights Amendment	48.2	12.7	v = .42***	39.7	19.8	v = .25***	18.5	10.8	v = .16**
Amendment to ban abortion	42.0	94.6	v = .56***	30.9	82.8	v = .46***	50.6	93.8	v = .46***
De-criminalization of marijuana use	10.9	3.2	v = .19***	16.9	13.9	v = .15**	7.8	4.7	v = .19***
Amendment to permit prayers and Bible reading in public schools	46.9	90.1	v = .47***	57.6	85.0	v = .25***	75.5	95.8	v = .28***
Domestic Economic Issues									
Across-the-board cuts in spending	77.9	83.2	v = .12**	72.9	74.2	v = .03	77.9	83.2	v = .07
Across-the-board tax increases	17.1	8.9	v = .12**	30.3	17.4	v = .13*	20.9	9.5	v = .20***
Public works program even if it means an increase in inflation	14.7	13.2	v = .04	12.0	14.8	v = .11*	11.0	6.4	v = .09
Environmental protection regulations	83.5	69.5	v = .18***	80.7	76.9	v = .04	72.9	72.3	v = .07
Foreign/Defense Issues									
Increased defense spending	47.8	72.7	v = .27***	50.0	58.0	v = .10	85.7	88.0	v = .05
Increased U.S. military presence in Middle East	32.3	47.9	v = .18***	26.6	51.6	v = .23***	45.8	56.5	v = .15**
Increased U.S. military presence in Latin America	46.6	68.6	v = .24***	45.4	66.9	v = .19***	75.1	77.7	v = .09
Intermediate-Range Nuclear-Force (INF) Treaty	76.8	32.8	v = .48***	78.7	45.8	v = .34***	65.9	26.3	v = .50***
Development of Strategic Defense Initiative (SDI)	74.5	88.8	v = .18***	70.5	76.9	v = .08	91.4	93.7	v = .07
(Minimum N)	(330)	(305)		(360)	(119)		(243)	(186)	

*Chi square statistically significant at .05 level
**Chi square statistically significant at .01 level
***Chi square statistically significant at .001 level

TABLE 3

Issue Positions of Bush Supporters, Robertson Supporters, and Democrats at 1988 State Conventions

	Maine			*South Carolina*		
	Bush Supporters (%)	Robertson Supporters (%)	Democrats (%)	Bush Supporters (%)	Robertson Supporters (%)	Democrats (%)
Domestic "Moral" Issues						
Equal Rights Amendment	39.7	19.8	90.9*	18.5	10.8	87.7*
Amendment to ban abortion	30.9	82.8	14.6	50.6	93.8	31.7
De-criminalization of marijuana use	16.9	13.9	51.3*	7.8	4.7	31.1*
Amendment to permit prayers and Bible reading in public schools	57.6	85.0	16.3*	75.5	95.8	52.3*
Domestic Economic Issues						
Across-the-board cuts in spending	72.9	74.2	32.3*	77.9	83.2	48.6*
Across-the-board tax increases	30.3	17.4	40.1	20.9	9.5	40.7*
Public works program even if it means an increase in inflation	12.0	14.8	50.9*	11.0	6.4	53.8*
Environmental protection regulations	80.7	76.9	97.7*	72.9	72.3	93.1*
Foreign/Defense Issues						
Increased defense spending	50.0	58.0	2.3*	85.7	88.0	9.7*
Increased U.S. military presence in Middle East	26.6	51.6	2.9	45.8	56.5	12.1*
Increased U.S. military presence in Latin America	45.4	66.9	3.1*	75.1	77.7	14.1*
Intermediate-Range Nuclear-Force (INF) Treaty	78.7	45.8	87.1	65.9	26.3	63.2
Development of Strategic Defense Initiative (SDI)	70.5	76.9	6.3*	91.4	93.7	25.1*
(Minimum N)	(360)	(119)	(788)	(243)	(186)	(613)

*Bush supporters closer to Robertson supporters than to Democrats

issues, Bush delegates in Maine were closer to the Robertson delegates than they were to the Maine Democratic delegates. In South Carolina, Bush and Robertson delegates were closer to each other than to Democratic delegates on eleven of thirteen policy issues. Thus, while these issue differences may produce intraparty tensions, it is unclear whether they are substantial enough to divide seriously the GOP or, at least, to prevent the forging of an electoral coalition to defeat Democrats.

Party Identification and Activity

The model of the professional partisan suggests that professionals tend to demonstrate relatively stable, long-term commitment to their party organization and its electoral success (Wilson 1962). Table 3 reveals that while majorities of both Bush and Robertson delegates classified themselves as "strong Republicans," Bush delegates were more likely to do so. Furthermore, Bush delegates were less likely to have switched parties. While large majorities of both Bush and Robertson delegates had been life-long Republicans, a significantly larger percentage of Robertson delegates had once considered themselves to be Democrats. Moreover, Robertson delegates who had switched parties were more likely to be recent converts. The lack of a stable, long-term commitment to their party and electoral success is also evident from the fact that Robertson supporters were generally less active in national political campaigns over the past decade than were Bush supporters.[6]

When the delegates were asked which of five different partisan activities they considered to be most important, "getting out the vote" received the greatest degree of support from all groups except Robertson supporters in Michigan (who ranked "getting out the vote" second). However, this limited consensus disappears when one examines other activities. In general, Robertson delegates proved far more likely than Bush delegates to rate "communicating issues" as most important.

The picture which emerges from this comparison conforms closely to popular perceptions of Robertson supporters as brash, issue-oriented amateurs who differed markedly from the more professional partisans supporting Bush. Of course, one must remember that some of the Bush delegates themselves were probably former amateurs, drawn into politics by enthusiasm for previous presidential candidates such as Barry Goldwater. Nevertheless, in view of the marked differences between Bush and Robertson supporters, it is hardly surprising that 1988 produced sharp conflict at state GOP conventions. But were these divisions long-lasting or have the Christian Right supporters of Robertson accommodated themselves to the GOP and been assimilated into the party? To answer this question we must examine the post-1988 activities of Robertson and his supporters.

---

[6] Exceedingly similar patterns also appear when one examines state and local campaign activity (see Penning 1992).

TABLE 4

Party Identification Political Activity of Bush and Robertson Supporters at 1988 State Republican Conventions

Characteristics:	Michigan			Maine			South Carolina		
	Bush Supporters (%)	Robertson Supporters (%)	Measure of Association	Bush Supporters (%)	Robertson Supporters (%)	Measure of Association	Bush Supporters (%)	Robertson Supporters (%)	Measure of Association
Strength of National Party ID									
Strong Republican	79.0	65.4		84.1	73.5		92.1	80.1	
Weak Republican	15.3	19.0	v = .20***	12.3	14.2	v = .17***	4.5	8.7	v = .18***
Ind./Republican or Ind.	5.7	15.7		3.6	12.4		3.4	11.2	
(N)	(333)	(306)		(365)	(113)		(265)	(196)	
Switched from Democrat to Republican?									
No	79.7	64.0	phi = .17***	83.5	72.6	phi = .12**	76.8	68.6	phi = .09*
Yes	20.3	36.0		16.5	27.4		23.2	31.4	
(N)	(340)	(314)		(376)	(124)		(263)	(194)	
Year in which Switch Occurred									
1979-1987	30.2	69.8		40.8	80.8		15.1	56.5	
1964-1978	41.5	19.8	v = .38***	42.9	11.5	v = .38**	39.6	28.3	v = .45***
Before 1964	28.3	10.5		16.3	7.7		45.3	15.2	
(N)	(53)	(86)		(49)	(26)		(53)	(46)	
National Election Campaigns									
Very actively worked	32.8	12.0		33.2	11.2		57.0	45.5	
Moderately worked	52.2	55.4	v = .28***	45.6	24.1	v = .41***	36.9	32.9	v = .23**
Not at all actively worked	15.0	32.6		21.1	64.7		6.0	21.6	
(N)	(314)	(267)		(331)	(116)		(249)	(167)	
Most Important Party Activity									
Getting Out the Vote	47.6	26.8		46.7	50.0		50.6	44.1	
(N)	(151)	(72)		(142)	(44)		(127)	(75)	
Communicating Issues	17.0	55.0		21.7	39.8		15.5	43.5	
(N)	(54)	(148)	v = .41***	(66)	(35)	v = .24***	(39)	(74)	v = .35***
Representing a Group	2.5	1.9		1.3	2.3		0.0	0.6	
(N)	(8)	(5)		(4)	(2)		(0)	(1)	
Recruiting Candidates	10.4	9.3		11.2	1.1		7.2	2.9	
(N)	(33)	(25)		(34)	(1)		(18)	(5)	
Building Party Organization	22.4	7.1		19.1	6.8		26.7	8.8	
(N)	(71)	(19)		(58)	(6)		(67)	(15)	

*Chi square statistically significant at .05 level
**Chi square statistically significant at .01 level
***Chi square statistically significant at .001 level

THE POST-1988 PERIOD

In 1981, Pat Robertson organized the Freedom Council, a nonpartisan citizens' organization designed to " 'encourage, train and equip Americans to exercise their civic responsibility to actively participate in politics'." During the first Reagan Administration, Robertson served as the Freedom Council's president and sought to use the group to organize his supporters at the grassroots level. However, the group had mixed success and was dissolved in 1986 amid an IRS investigation over its tax-exempt status (Moen 1992:37-38).

Following his failed 1988 bid for the GOP presidential nomination, Pat Robertson admitted making a fundamental campaign error, namely, spending too much money on building grassroots organizations and too little on mass media advertising (Hertzke 1993:170).[7] Ironically, however, this error may have worked to his long-run advantage by facilitating post-election efforts to organize his supporters into a new and more effective political force at the state and local levels. In 1989, building on the foundation created by the Freedom Council and his campaign organization, Robertson organized the Christian Coalition, a nonpartisan organization designed to promote his "pro-family" political agenda, including choice in education, reforming school curricula (e.g., opposing sex education), opposing abortion, supporting tax cuts, and getting tough on crime (Beck 1992:22-26; Miller 1992:A9). In addition, the Christian Coalition vigorously opposes pornography (Johnson 1990), feminism (Isikoff 1992), and gay rights — including gays in the military (Associated Press 1992).

The Christian Coalition is headed by Ralph Reed, Jr., an intelligent, energetic, and highly articulate spokesman. Reed, a former executive director of the College Republican National Committee, experienced a dramatic "conversion" one evening while drinking beer with friends at a Capitol Hill bar called Bullfeathers. According to Reed, he had a vision in which he saw death awaiting his friends and him if he failed to mend his ways. Reed rushed to a telephone and contacted the first church he saw listed in the directory. Reed reports that, "My conversion was pretty dramatic. Now I'm where I think God wants me to be" (Perry 1992).

Among the Christian Coalition's first political activities was its largely unsuccessful effort in 1990 to eliminate funding for the National Endowment for the Arts through lobbying Congress and targeting seven key congressmen for electoral defeat (Johnson 1990). Its first major political victory occurred in the same year when the Coalition, in cooperation with conservative Catholics, contributed to the defeat of a gay-rights ordinance in Broward County, Florida (Perry 1992). This helped to establish a pattern in which the Christian Coalition has worked in cooperation with kindred groups in order to achieve its political objectives.

---

[7] In this sense, Robertson's efforts differ significantly from those of certain other Christian Right leaders such as the Rev. Jerry Falwell who tended to rely heavily, if not exclusively, on making appeals through the media.

Pat Robertson calls the Christian Coalition the fastest growing independent political organization in the United States (Hertzke 1993:17), and he may well be correct. In four years, the Coalition has enlisted 350,000 members nationwide (Connell 1993), and its bimonthly newspaper, *Christian America*, has attracted 200,000 subscribers. The Coalition, based in Chesapeake, Virginia, is organizationally unrelated to other Robertson operations in nearby Virginia Beach. Coalition spokespersons report that the organization has a staff of 30 and an annual budget of more than $4.3 million (Beck 1992:21-22). Currently, the Christian Coalition maintains over 750 chapters and operates in all 50 states (Russell, 1993).

Although budget and membership data are informative, the key to the Christian Coalition's political effectiveness lies in the commitment of its membership and in the well-conceived strategy and tactics developed by its leaders. The basic coalition strategy is epitomized by its motto, "Think like Jesus . . . run like Lincoln." To Coalition leaders, "running like Lincoln" means grassroots organization — building structures that identify sympathetic voters in states and localities, and mobilize them on election day. Toward this end, Coalition leaders have developed political "stealth" tactics, sometimes compared to "flying below radar" (San Francisco Chronicle 1992). Stealth campaigns are conducted in a nontraditional manner, with a conscious attempt to avoid publicity. Little-known candidates run for office and eschew advertising on television, attending candidate forums, and responding to press inquiries. Instead, they concentrate on ferociously organizing their supporters in churches and related Christian groups. Among the most important activities undertaken by stealth campaigners is conducting telephone surveys to identify supporters (Beck 1992:22). In addition, the Coalition conducts "in-pew" voter registration and distributes voter guides rating candidates on issues (Isikoff 1991). The massive scale of these efforts is illustrated by Coalition efforts to distribute 40 million voter guides in 246,000 churches in 1992. According to Robertson, this distribution was "the most comprehensive effort in the history of the country" (Applebome 1992).

The 1992 Elections

The Christian Coalition was exceedingly active in local, state, and national campaigns during the critical election year, 1992. Not only did the organization engage in the massive distribution of voter guides, noted above, but it also devoted substantial resources to candidate recruitment and leadership training. In its first two years of existence, the Coalition trained 5,000 leaders at its Virginia headquarters. For 1992, the goal was to train 5,000 to 10,000 more (Perry 1992). Furthermore, prior to the 1992 campaign, the Coalition brought together over 1,000 ministers and other supporters to plan strategy to register voters, get out the vote, and influence the Republican party (Hertzke 1993:2).

The goals of the Coalition's state and local efforts in 1992 were exceedingly diverse, ranging from electing school board members to influencing the fate of statewide propositions. Although it is difficult to assess the impact of Coalition efforts accurately, after the election the Coalition could point to some remarkable successes at the state and local levels. According to the liberal lobbying group, People For the American Way (Mydans 1992), fundamentalist Christians won about 40 percent of the 500 electoral contests it monitored nationwide. Ralph Reed indicated that while his organization had not done its own calculations, he agreed with this overall assessment. According to Reed,

> We focused on where the real power is: in the states and in the precincts and in the neighborhoods where people live and work. . . . On the one hand, George Bush was going down to ignominious defeat in a landslide. On the other hand, the anecdotal evidence is that at school boards and at the state legislative level we had big, tremendous victories.

Although the fiercest battleground was California, the Coalition also worked exceedingly hard and did well in Iowa, Kansas, Florida, and Texas. The Coalition scored impressive victories in Iowa, for example, where according to People for the American Way, the Christian Right won two Congressional seats as well as 6 out of the 12 state legislative races in which they campaigned. The Coalition also contributed to the narrow defeat, 52 percent to 48 percent, of an Iowa initiative that would have created a state version of the Equal Rights Amendment (Perry 1992:A16). Other Coalition successes occurred in both Colorado and Tampa, Florida, where gay rights laws were overturned.

One of the Coalition's most notable victories occurred in South Carolina, where little-known lawyer, Bob Inglis, defeated seemingly unbeatable three-term Democratic United States Representative, Liz Patterson. Although Inglis denied being a "stealth" candidate (Hoover 1992b), he ran a campaign "rooted in secrecy, an occasional ruse, short on confrontation, long on shoe leather, and an alliance with increasingly politicized Christian conservatives. . . . I don't think Congresswoman Patterson ever understood just how much we were doing," claimed Inglis, "They just thought it was nothing" (Hoover 1992a). At least part of the credit for Inglis's stunning upset must go to the Christian Coalition. Although, in keeping with its policy, the Coalition did not directly endorse candidate Inglis, it did make available voter guides, clarifying the issues and candidate positions. Indeed, less than 48 hours before the election, 840,000 voter guides were inserted in church bulletins across South Carolina. In Patterson's district, 200,000 bulletins were stuffed in 700 churches. Roberta Combs of Charleston, the Christian Coalition's state coordinator, contended that these efforts were "very effective" in helping to secure the Inglis victory (Hoover 1992b).

On the other hand, the Coalition also suffered a number of defeats. It was unable to secure voter approval of a proposed amendment to the Oregon state constitution that would have required public schools to teach that homosexuality is "abnormal, wrong, unnatural, and perverse" (Perry 1992). And in San Diego, California a massive counterattack by Coalition opponents reversed previous Coalition gains. In 1990, candidates from the Christian Right had succeeded in electing 60 out of a slate of 88 candidates for local offices. However, two years later, opponents developed a highly successful tactic of publicizing the Christian Right-backed candidates' positions, hoping voters would reject their agenda once it became known. Ken Blalack, a Republican heading a group called Community for Responsible Education which was formed to oppose the stealth candidates reported that "We are one happy bunch. . . . We won well over two out of three seats here in San Diego County" (Mydans 1992).

Christian Coalition supporters and other members of the Christian Right also played a prominent role in the presidential election, most notably at the 1992 Republican national convention. Bush-Quayle campaign officials estimated that more than 40 percent of all the delegates to the Convention were evangelical Christians.[8] Moreover, Christian Coalition officials estimated that 300 of the approximately 2,000 delegates were members of Christian Coalition (Lawton 1992a:51). Other estimates placed Christian Coalition representation as high as 20 percent of the total (Lehmann 1992:10). Of the 107 delegates who served on the GOP platform drafting committee, 21 were members of the Christian Coalition (Hertzke 1993:184). At the platform hearings, Ralph Reed argued strongly for an anti-abortion plank and an emphasis on "family values" in the GOP platform. According to Reed, in 1988 some twenty-four million voters identified themselves as "born-again" Christians or pro-life Catholics, a crucial voting bloc that provided Bush with nearly 90 percent of his support (Hertzke 1993:171). Reed and other supporters of the Christian Right proved highly successful in their efforts, securing approval of a conservative GOP platform which included "acknowledgement of a belief in God, a staunch prolife plank, opposition to gay rights, support for educational choice and school prayer, opposition to the distribution of condoms in schools, and a pledge to fight pornography" (Lawton 1992a:51).

Robertson, the Christian Coalition, and the Future of the GOP

In the 1992 presidential election, George Bush was able to win majorities among only two demographic groups — persons making over $100,000 per year and white evangelical Christians. A Christian Coalition poll revealed that 55 percent of self-identified white evangelicals voted for Bush, 28 percent for Clinton, and 17 percent for Ross Perot. John Green of the University of Akron points out that "If you compare 55 percent with the 38 percent of the general population who voted for Bush, there was a very dramatic level of support from evangelicals." According to Green, that loyalty, coupled with high evangelical turnout, has made evangelicals "the central voting bloc in the GOP" (Lawton 1992b:41).

Yet certain Republican moderates, far from praising members of the Christian Right for their support of Bush, blame them for his defeat. According to former congressman Peter Smith, president of the moderate Republican Ripon Society, "The ultimate betrayal of Bush will be to say he wasn't conservative enough. . . . It was, in fact, the embracing of his [conservative] platform at the convention that sealed the president's doom." Similarly, Bush Labor Secretary,

---

[8] The percentage of evangelicals among GOP rank-and-file identifiers varies, depending on one's definition of the term, "evangelical." The 1988 University of Michigan National Election Study reveals that (1) 38.8 percent of GOP identifiers classified themselves as "born again Christians," (2) 34.6 percent classified themselves as both "born again Christians" and "Protestants," and (3) 22.8 percent classified themselves as "born again Christians" and "Protestants" and also agreed that "The Bible is God's word and all it says is true."

Lynn Martin, asserted that "We can't appeal to a narrow group of voters and merely attempt to secure a base that . . . doesn't move us to a wider group of voters who have their natural home in the Republican Party" (Eicher 1992:6). On the other hand, conservatives refused to accept the blame for Bush's defeat, arguing that Bush's poor performance in office and lack of ideological vision were the primary contributing factors.

It is, of course, common for party members to point fingers after a humiliating electoral defeat. But the current degree of bitterness and division may prove exceedingly difficult to eliminate. In part this is because, as noted above, Christian Right supporters and traditional Republicans differ markedly in terms of political experience, ideology, issue positions, and world views. It may also reflect the well-founded fears of traditional Republicans that newcomers are trying to take over the party. In Kansas City, for example, Christian Right efforts to gain control nearly produced a "civil war" and has created a party without direction. Jackson County GOP Chairman, Gary Martinette, complained that "The party right now is like an animal whose head's been cut off — flailing around until it finds a new direction or grows a new head" (Montgomery 1992). Similar complaints come from John Treen, GOP Chairman in Jefferson Parish, Louisiana, who estimated that more than half of the GOP's central committee in Louisiana is now in the hands of Christian Coalition members. According to Treen, "What they're doing is antagonizing the hell out of mainstream Republicans who have just gotten fed up" (Isikoff 1991). Tensions have run high in Michigan as well, where traditional Republicans have expressed concern over Christian Right efforts to insert planks in the state party platform opposing both sex education in the schools and domestic partners legislation. As a result, the moderates have changed party rules to provide that at post-1993 Republican state conventions the party platform committee will be selected by the state chairman.

The dilemma faced by the Republican Party is that Christian Coalition members and other conservative Christians constitute arguably the most active component of the party. Efforts to drive them out of the GOP might leave the party moribund. Perhaps that is why certain party supporters are calling for unity and assimilation. According to Fred Barnes, an evangelical and political writer for the *New Republic*, the "worst thing" that could happen to Republicans is for party regulars is to view the Christian Right as a "threat to the party . . . [that] needs to be driven out in some kind of civil war" (Eicher 1992:7). And former GOP congressman Vin Weber argues that when evangelical Christians do become involved in the party, "they become good Republican activists. They become deal-cutters themselves" (Perry 1992). Indeed, there is some evidence to support this position. Immediately following the 1992 presidential election, Ralph Reed suggested that the Christian Coalition and its allies will have to accept a diverse array of views. "That will be our challenge," argued Reed, "to temper our message of conviction with a counterbalance of diversity and tolerance. . . . We will convey to people that we believe certain things strongly but accept and welcome a diversity of views" (Miller 1992:A9). If this does happen, the Robertson phenomenon may, ultimately, provide net benefits for the Republican party. But few believe that the task of unifying the party will be easy.

CONCLUSIONS

Pat Robertson's 1988 presidential campaign raised concerns over the possibility that an infusion of "amateur" ideologues into party affairs would cause intraparty conflict and weaken party efforts to build coalitions and win elections. To a substantial degree, this study demonstrates the validity of these concerns. The responses of Bush and Robertson delegates in Michigan, Maine, and South Carolina reveal remarkably similar patterns, with Robertson supporters tending to appear generally more "amateurish" and less "professional" than Bush supporters. Moreover, important issue disagreements were found between the two groups of delegates, particularly with respect to "moral" issues such as abortion and prayer and Bible reading in public schools.

Post-1988 events also suggest that the Robertson phenomenon has seriously divided the Republican Party. Robertson's Christian Coalition supporters have worked exceedingly hard and effectively to win leadership positions within the GOP and to incorporate their conservative agenda into the party platform. The predictable result has been bitterness and strife within the party.

Do these findings suggest that the religious right is likely to generate extreme factionalism within the Republican party in the near future and that the GOP will be unable to unify itself sufficiently to compete successfully against the Democratic Party? To some degree, the answer may be "yes." Certainly, the divisions between traditional and Christian Right Republicans are significant. Furthermore, support for the Republican party does appear to be more conditional among Robertson supporters than among more traditional Republicans.

Yet one must be cautious in pronouncing doom upon the GOP. For one thing, the election of Democrat Bill Clinton to the presidency has provided both traditional Republicans and Christian Right newcomers with a common "enemy." According to Ralph Reed, the Clinton victory is likely to energize Clinton's opponents, arguing that "for Christians, without a crucifixion, there's no resurrection" (Bandy 1992). In addition, there may well be a tendency for the most extreme activists to withdraw from partisan activity immediately following an electoral defeat, leaving a group of remaining newcomers who are relatively willing to come to terms with party regulars. In Maine, for example, party officials have reported that while some of the most committed Robertson delegates have indeed decided to forego additional party activity, those Robertson supporters who have remained in the party have made solid contributions. Moreover, Ralph Reed's recognition of the need to tolerate intraparty diversity offers hope for those who seek GOP unity.

Like the findings of Green and Guth (1988), this study's findings suggest that, despite major differences between Robertson newcomers and Bush regulars, accommodation and assimilation could well occur.[9] Disagreements between the two groups will certainly continue to produce serious intraparty friction, particu-

---

[9] Hertzke (1989) points out that this assimilation has been smoother at the national level than at the state level. At the state level, the Robertson assimilation has varied from state-to-date, depending on the degree to which his supporters have sought to dominate the party.

larly if Robertson or a Robertson-like candidate should choose to run for president in future campaigns. Yet the differences between the two groups appear to be smaller than those dividing each of them from the Democratic party. Thus, over time the Robertson candidacy may benefit the GOP by injecting a new group of enthusiastic and relatively youthful activists into the party.

REFERENCES

Applebome, P. 1992. "Religious right intensifies campaign for Bush." *New York Times* (Oct. 30): A1.

Associated Press. 1993. "Gays-in-military issue helps fill up fund-raisers' direct-mail bags." *Grand Rapids Press* (Feb. 27): A14.

Baker, T. A., R. P. Steed, and L. W. Moreland. 1991. "Preachers and politics," pp. 94-112 in James L. Guth and John C. Green (eds.), *The Bible and the Ballot Box*. Boulder, CO: Westview.

Bandy, L. 1992. "Now outside the camp, Christian right likely to prosper." *Greenville News* (Nov. 23): 5A.

Barnes, F. 1986. "Rarin' to go." *New Republic* (Sept. 29): 14-15.

Beck, R. 1992. "Washington's profamily activists." *Christianity Today* (Nov. 9): 20-28.

Church, G. 1986. "Keeping the faith." *Time* (Aug. 18): 14-16.

Connell, J. 1993. "Christian Coalition aide is a Jew with a mission." *Grand Rapids Press* (Mar. 21): A6.

Dionne, E. J., Jr. 1988. "Michigan GOP is split on eve of vote." *New York Times* (Jan. 14): A20.

Eicher, N. S. 1992. "Beyond the blame game." *World* (Nov. 14): 6-7.

Eldersveld, S. J. 1964. *Political Parties*. Chicago: Rand McNally.

Green, J. C. and J. L. Guth. 1988. "The Christian right in the Republican party." *Journal of Politics* 50:150-65.

Guth, J. L. and J. C. Green. 1987. "The GOP and the Christian right." Paper presented at the annual meeting of the Midwest Political Science Association, Chicago, Apr. 9-11.

Hauss, C. and L. S. Maisel. 1986. "Extremist delegates," pp. 215-26 in R. Rapoport, A. Abramowitz, and J. McGlennon (eds.), *The Life of the Parties*. Lexington: University of Kentucky Press.

Hertzke, Alan. 1989. "Pat Robertson's crusade and the GOP." Paper presented at the annual meeting of the Midwest Political Science Association, Chicago, Apr. 13-15.

_____. 1993. *Echoes of Discontent*. Washington, DC: Congressional Quarterly Press.

Hoover, D. 1992a. "Shoe leather, secrecy, Christian Coalition helped." *Greenville News* (Nov. 5): 1A.

_____. 1992b. "Robertson backers renew political muscle-flexing with Christian Coalition." *Greenville News* (Nov. 8): 1A.

Hornbeck, M. and E. Petykiewicz. 1988. "Bush holds lead in bitter GOP battles." *Grand Rapids Press* (Jan. 15): A1-2.

Isikoff, M. 1992. "Powerful Christian Coalition has grip on GOP's grass roots." *Grand Rapids Press* (Sept. 13): A8.

Johnson, D. 1990. "Group links pornography support to lawmakers' vote on art funds." *New York Times* (Nov. 3): I11.

Kessell, J. 1988. *Presidential Campaign Politics*, 3rd ed. Chicago: Dorsey Press.

Kirkpatrick, J. 1976. *The New Presidential Elite*. New York: Russell Sage.

Lawton, K. A. 1992a. "A Republican God?" *Christianity Today* (Oct. 5): 50-52.

_____. 1992b. "Seeking common ground." *Christianity Today* (Dec. 14): 40-41, 62.

Lehmann, D. J. 1992. "Evangelicals say stakes are high for GOP." *Chicago Sun-Times* (Oct. 4): 10.

Miller, A. C. 1992. "Faction digs in at bottom." *Kansas City Star* (Nov. 23): A8-9.

Moen, M. C. 1992. *The Transformation of the Christian Right*. Tuscaloosa: University of Alabama Press.

Montgomery, R. 1992. "Christian right tries grass-roots plan." *Kansas City Star* (Nov. 23): A8.

McGlennon, J. 1989. "Religious activists in the Republican party." Paper presented at the annual meeting of the Midwest Political Science Association, Chicago, Apr. 13-15.

Mydans, S. 1992. "Christian conservatives counting hundreds of gains in local votes.' *New York Times* (Nov. 21): A1.

Oldfield, D. 1988. "Pat crashes the party." Paper presented at the annual meeting of the American Political Science Association, Washington, DC, Sept. 1-4.

Penning. J. M. 1992. "Support for Bush and Robertson among GOP activists." Paper presented at The Citadel Symposium on Southern Politics, Charleston, SC, Mar. 5-6.

Perry, J. M. 1992. "Christian right maps route to power in efforts at the local level to oppose homosexual rights." *Wall Street Journal* (Nov. 25): A16.

Phillips, L. 1988. "Born-again push to 'vote for the real thing'." *USA Today* (Jul. 15): 1A.

Ranney, A. 1975. *Curing the Mischiefs of Faction*. Berkeley: University of California Press.

Russell, M. 1993. Christian Coalition communications director, interview. Mar. 22.

San Francisco Chronicle. 1992. "Observers: evangelicals' support for GOP a mixed blessing." *San Francisco Chronicle* (Nov. 9): A10.

Smidt, C. and J. M. Penning. 1990. "A party divided?" *Polity* 23: 129-38.

Sorauf, F. J. and P. A. Beck. 1988. *Party Politics in America*. Glenview, IL: Scott Foresman/Little Brown.

Wilcox, C. 1991. *God's Warriors*. Baltimore, MD: Johns Hopkins University Press.

Wilkerson, R., T. Sypert, and E. Slowik. 1988. "2 candidates claim win in chaotic GOP." *Grand Rapids Press* (Jan. 29): A1, A6.

Wilson, J. Q. 1962. *The Amateur Democrat*. Chicago: University of Chicago Press.

8

From Revolution to Evolution: The Changing Nature of the Christian Right

Matthew C. Moen
University of Maine

This interpretive chapter examines major organizational and tactical changes in the Christian Right, from its origin in the late 1970s to the present. It argues that the Christian Right has passed through several distinctive phases, gradually becoming much more of a traditional political actor following conventional strategies in American politics. This chapter also examines popular and scholarly understanding of the movement's rise and evolution, with special attention to paradigms impeding understanding of the Christian Right. It closes with suggestions for further research.

The principal objective of this chapter is to explain change in the Christian Right over time; the central argument is that the Christian Right has gradually reconciled and adjusted itself to the secular norms and practices of American politics. Stated alliteratively, the Christian Right has forsaken revolution for evolution, abandoning its quixotic quest to "put God back in government" (Ogintz 1980) for a calculated campaign to infiltrate and influence carefully selected repositories of political power. It has done so on its own rhythm, rather than on the cycle of presidential politics, as one might reasonably surmise from the exhaustive research on the presidential elections of the 1980s and 1992 (Johnson and Tamney 1982; Smidt 1983, 1987; Miller and Wattenberg 1984; Himmelstein and McRae 1984; Brudney and Copeland 1984, 1988; Buell and Sigelman 1985; Sigelman et al. 1987; Wilcox 1987; Jelen 1987; Guth and Green 1991; Kellstedt et al. 1990; Green 1993; Leege 1993; Kellstedt et al. 1993; Johnson et al. 1993).

With a few exceptions (Lienesch 1982; Bruce 1988; Moen 1992), scholars have not really focused on how political activism has shaped the Christian Right, preferring instead to concentrate on how the Christian Right has influenced politics. Neglecting one side of that causal relationship has skewed the literature; scholars know much about the Christian Right's voting behavior, campaigning, and lobbying, but comparatively little about its internal dynamics over time. Yet, it is important to understand the movement's machinations, both for the sake of explanation and prognostication. This chapter is a small step in that direction; I deliberately sketch the big picture, providing references along the way to works containing the details.

A subsidiary objective of this essay is to examine popular and scholarly understanding of the Christian Right. This task is approached in a constructive spirit, with the hope of fostering dialogue among scholars; it is not meant to suggest that only my interpretations are correct, nor to replicate solid review essays of the existing literature (Guth *et al.* 1988; Hertzke 1988a). The time is ripe to assess the state of affairs, in the wake of the Reagan-Bush era and of events that captured the attention of scholars, such as the closure of Moral Majority (Hadden *et al.* 1987; Hadden and Shupe 1988; Bledsoe 1990) and the candidacy of Pat Robertson (Guth and Green 1991; Langenbach 1988; Green and Guth 1988; Johnson *et al.* 1989; Green 1993; Hertzke 1993). Many words were penned about the Christian Right during the 1980s and the 1992 elections, making it an opportune time to reflect on some of the things written.

THE RISE OF THE CHRISTIAN RIGHT

The rapid rise of the Christian Right in the late 1970s astonished observers of American politics. Journalists were among the most surprised, writing only two articles during the time the movement was crystallizing (March 1979-February 1980), as measured by the *Reader's Guide to Periodical Literature*. Many politicians were also caught off guard. The "born-again" Baptist president, Jimmy Carter, did not sense the depth of unrest among conservative Christians until it became too late to make amends (Hastey 1981). The whole situation was aptly described years later by Kenneth D. Wald (1987:182): "Of all the shifts and surprises in contemporary political life, perhaps none was so wholly unexpected as the political resurgence of evangelical Protestantism in the 1970s."

The rise of the Christian Right is a familiar story that has been told by historians, sociologists, theologians, and political scientists, among others (Jorstad 1981; Kater 1982; Liebman and Wuthnow 1983; Bromley and Shupe 1984; Bruce 1987; Wald 1987). Common to those discussions is that the Christian Right arose in response to a complex array of liberal and secular trends, ranging from the eradication of religion in the schools, to easy availability of abortion, to tax policies that adversely affected the traditional family.

The rapid rise of the Christian Right spawned a potent and sometimes mean-spirited counterattack from those far removed from the conservative Christian subculture. Liberal activists created groups like People For the American Way as platforms for personal attacks on Christian Right leaders; intellectuals mocked the Christian Right's concerns by penning a "Secular Humanist Declaration"; theologians drew unflattering biblical analogies, with the Rev. William Sloan Coffin suggesting that Christian Right leaders were "jackasses"; government officials reflexively described Moral Majority as a white racist group, and compared Jerry Falwell to the Ayatollah Khomeni, as if one could casually ignore the legal, cultural, and theological schisms separating an American Christian from an Iranian Muslim (Nyhan 1980; Unger 1980; Hyer 1980; Briggs 1981; "Christian Right" 1980). Scholars opposed to the Christian Right also succumbed to the temptation to overstate matters, with one historian comparing the Christian Right of the 1970s to the European Fascism of the 1940s (Linder 1982). The shrill rhetoric and simplistic comparisons shaped the tone of public discourse in the early 1980s, just as opponents hoped. The Christian Right was caricatured as a collection of hillbillies bent on creating a theocracy, and evidence that this view was assimilated by the public could be found in its negative assessment of the Christian Right's leaders, issues, and organizations (Shupe and Stacey 1983; Buell and Sigelman 1985; Wilcox 1987; Sigelman *et al.* 1987; Guth and Green 1987).

Researchers certainly did not create the negative perceptions that took root; the Christian Right's opponents and even its own leaders accomplished that task, through their miscalculations and mistakes (Moen 1989). Yet, once scholars started explaining the rise of the Christian Right, they contributed to the perception that the movement was suspect. Hadden and Swann (1981) laid the groundwork for many subsequent studies by suggesting that the Christian Right was a technologically driven movement spawned by master manipulators. They identified the modern "televangelist" as the force behind the surge of traditional religiosity. While a plausible explanation, it blinded other observers to the possibility that the Christian Right was more of a grassroots protest than a technological artifact; moreover, such a "top down" explanation implicitly trivialized the concerns of social conservatives, by casting those concerns as the baggage of unsophisticated followers being duped by clever elites.

Journalists subsequently portrayed the "televangelist" label and the "top down" paradigm as gospel, occupying themselves with unmasking the conservative preacher conspiracy afoot. Their work reached its apogee years later, when they blithely associated ministers barely connected to the Christian Right but tainted by scandal, such as Jim Bakker and Oral Roberts, with those responsible for creating the key Christian Right groups (Marz *et al.* 1987; Ostling 1987). Many journalists never grasped the distinctions among ministries and objectives, equating Jim Bakker's quest to build the ultimate pentecostal amusement park with fundamentalist Jerry Falwell's mission to remake America. (Some still insist on stereotyping conservative Christians, demonstrated by a *Washington Post* article calling evangelicals "uneducated and easy to command"; see Morin 1993). Given this lack of understanding of the conservative Christian community, and the inculcation of the "top down" paradigm, is it any wonder that the "resurgence" of the Christian Right circa 1992 surprised many writers?

Scholars fed the perception that the Christian Right was suspect in another way — by using frameworks that suggested some sort of personal or social strain. For instance, Wald and his colleagues (1989a) borrowed from the psychology literature to examine empirical support for "authority-mindedness" in the Christian Right; other scholars used the status politics and life-style defense paradigms toward a similar end (Crawford 1980; Lorentzen 1980; Lipset 1982; Conover 1983; Harper and Leicht 1984; Wald *et al.* 1989b). Those paradigms drew criticism for their explanatory power (Simpson 1983; Miller 1985; Moen 1988; Smidt 1988), and also for their presumption of pathological problems among Christian Right supporters (Jelen 1991; Wilcox 1992).

The larger point is that the Christian Right was placed very early into established frameworks that often reflected a liberal understanding of the conservative mindset. The concerns of Christian Right supporters were explained as the by-product of authoritarian personalities or symbolic crusades, rather than taken at face value. One unfortunate result of pigeonholing the Christian Right was that scholars circumscribed their research agendas. They neglected fruitful lines of inquiry, while debating the fine points of value-laden frameworks — the academic equivalent of fiddling while Rome burned. For instance, scholars virtually ignored the Christian Right's infiltration of state Republican party organizations until the Reagan era was over (see Morken 1990; Oldfield 1990, 1992; Hertzke 1993). Those missed opportunities are not easily recompensed because the Christian Right has undergone dramatic changes over time.

PERIODS OF DEVELOPMENT

The Christian Right has passed through two distinctive phases since its rise in the late-1970s, and is in the midst of a third (Moen 1992). This periodization scheme is embellished and refined here to provide a picture of how the Christian Right has evolved. While such a framework is open to criticism, it may serve to synthesize major changes in the Christian Right, including its reorientation to the traditional norms and practices of American politics.

Expansionist Period (1978-1984)

As the label implies, the dominant characteristic of the Christian Right during the expansionist period was steady growth. The National Christian Action Coalition was launched in 1978 and became the first national organization of the Christian Right. It was followed by the Religious Roundtable, Christian Voice, Moral Majority, and Concerned Women for America (1979), the Freedom Council (1981), and the American Coalition for Traditional Values (1983). The proliferation of organizations and their concomitant division of labor signaled steady growth (Hatch 1983).

Reliable membership estimates for each specific organization were difficult to obtain. Christian Right leaders dispensed data, but they had every incentive to exaggerate their constituency's size. Independent assessments varied considerably. With Moral Majority, for instance, scholars suggested membership figures that ranged from 482,000 to 3,000,000; journalists estimated its voter registration campaigns netted 200,000 to 3,000,000 new voters (Liebman 1983; Hadden et al. 1987; Wald 1987; Spring 1984; Harwood 1985). When scholars documented the unpopularity of Moral Majority's issue positions, they implicitly confirmed the lower estimates, although they mostly refrained from such conjecture (Shupe and Stacey 1983; Buell and Sigelman 1985; Wilcox 1987; Sigelman et al. 1987; Guth and Green 1987). Based on Moral Majority alone, though, one can reasonably conclude that the Christian Right consisted of several hundred thousand (if not millions of) citizens. It grew at a remarkable rate early on.

The geometric growth of the Christian Right created a high public profile. Journalists wrote hundreds of stories about its leaders and organizations (Hadden and Shupe 1988), with 75 percent of that coverage coming within three years after an organization was launched (Moen 1992). Since seven of the eleven national organizations composing the Christian Right formed during the expansionist period, the early 1980s were a publicity bonanza.

Owing to rapid growth and high visibility, the Christian Right successfully influenced the political agenda. It helped shift the congressional agenda in fundamental ways, winning votes on constitutional amendments to ban abortion and to permit prayer in schools in the 98th Congress (1983-1984), as well as securing passage of an array of lesser objectives (Hertzke 1988b; Moen 1989). It also altered the public dialogue. The Christian Right placed a cluster of issues involving conventional morality and the traditional family at the political forefront, simultaneously bumping off items that offended, such as the Equal Rights Amendment (Hadden and Shupe 1988; Hofrenning 1989; Dionne 1989; Wald 1992). Some observers missed those indices of influence. Pressman (1984) and D'Antonio (1990), for instance, defined success for the Christian Right in absolute rather than relative terms — it should win elections and final passage of bills, not just alter the terms of debate. Those questionable standards contributed to the erroneous assessment that the Christian Right was spent by the mid-1980s.

Ironically, the Christian Right's agenda-setting success was costly. It convinced many lawmakers that it was time to consider new issues, since key Christian Right objectives were voted upon in the 98th Congress (1983-1984). Concurrently, Christian Right leaders made a host of mistakes while lobbying on Capitol Hill that created a less hospitable environment in the future. Their political amateurishness was yet another defining characteristic of the expansionist period, and it abetted the demise of the early groups.

The expansionist period is also distinguishable by the overt and pervasive religious underpinnings of the Christian Right. It was led by a clique of fundamentalist pastors and laypersons, such as Bob Billings (National Christian Action Coalition), Ed McAteer (Religious Roundtable), Jerry Falwell (Moral Majority), Beverly LaHaye (Concerned Women for America), and Tim LaHaye (American Coalition for Traditional Values). They attracted mostly fundamentalist supporters, who were very conservative and often intolerant of their evangelical and pentecostal brethren (Shupe and Stacey 1983; Wilcox 1986, 1989; Beatty and Walter 1988). The presence of fundamentalists was most evident at the 1980 National Affairs Briefing, where leaders made pronouncements grounded in a literal interpretation of the Bible that jarred many Americans, such as God not hearing the prayers of Jews (Jorstad 1981).

The predominance of fundamentalists during the expansionist period was also evident in the way that leaders handled political issues. They focused on issues with strong moral overtones, such as gay rights, abortion, and pornography; moreover, they declared the correct position on those issues according to Scripture, and attacked alternative views as misguided biblical interpretation or secularism (Heinz 1983). Christian Right leaders also used moralistic language, speaking freely about the need to restore "moral sanity" (Falwell 1980), and defining issues like abortion and pornography in terms of sin. Taking stock of the Christian Right's rhetoric and early activities, Jorstad (1981:8) stated: "The theme brought home in every speech, every sermon, every pamphlet, every request for funds was that of saving Americans by a return to what the leaders called its traditional morality." The early Christian Right was long on morality, but short on skill.

Transition Period (1965-1986)

The critical transition period is often overlooked by scholars intent on explaining the rise of the Christian Right in the early 1980s or assessing its activities in the wake of Moral Majority and Pat Robertson's presidential bid. The distinguishing feature of this period was retrenchment. Table 1 chronicles the fate of the early organizations during this time.

TABLE 1

Retrenchment Among Christian Right Organizations: 1985-1986

Organization	Status	Action by Group Leader
National Christian Action Coalition	dissolved	Bill Billings quits politics
Religious Roundtable	moribund	Ed McAteer runs for Tennessee Senate seat in 1984
Christian Voice	moribund	Robert Grant departs to lead American Freedom Coalition
Moral Majority	dissolved	Jerry Falwell merges group into Liberty Federation
Concerned Women for America	relocated	Beverly LaHaye moves from San Diego to Washington, D.C.
Freedom Council	dissolved	Pat Robertson dissolves group amidst IRS audit
American Coalition for Traditional Values	dissolved	Tim LaHaye dissolves group following allegations of a tie to the Rev. Moon

The breadth of change is striking. Nearly every organization suspended its work, merged with another, or dissolved. (The only new group formed during this time was the Liberty Federation in 1986, which was Jerry Falwell's vehicle for absorbing the Moral Majority and then exiting politics in 1987.) The principal reason for retrenchment was the erosion of a direct-mail base during the mid-1980s (Diamond 1989:59). It was caused by an odd combination of agenda-setting successes that defused the anger of conservative Christians, along with tactical blunders that sapped their confidence in their leaders. Local supporters became weary of constant monetary appeals to fight distant national battles (Moen 1992:27).

Interestingly, this wholesale transformation went virtually unnoticed. The *New York Times* carried only 16 stories about the Christian Right during the transition period (focused mostly on Pat Robertson's budding presidential candidacy), compared to 132 stories in 1980-1981. The decreased visibility seemed to reflect the institutionalization of the "top down" and symbolic crusade paradigms, which assumed that Christian Right supporters would decrease their activism once they vented their frustrations. The media was so certain that the Christian Right was fading away that it paid scant attention at all, let alone to subtle changes in progress.

As in the expansionist period, one change fostered others. The organizational retrenchment eradicated natural platforms for Christian Right leaders to speak out on issues, and consequently eroded their ability to shape the legislative and public agendas. The retrenchment also destroyed some of the inventiveness that the Christian Right exhibited in its earliest years, when it was on the cutting edge of issues, such as the impact of the tax code on families and the quality of the public schools. Christian Right leaders were relegated to the role of apologists for controversial Reagan-administration positions, including South African sanctions and aid to the Nicaraguan Contras. The movement's agenda withered along with its early organizations, tempting observers to write a political obituary. Yet, Christian Right leaders were using this time of retrenchment to advance a strategic reorientation already in progress. The rapid collapse of organizations and a political agenda simply hastened that process.

Institutionalization Period (1987-present)

The distinguishing feature of the institutionalization period is the existence of several stable and well-positioned organizations. Space constraints preclude a discussion of the role of Christian Right elites in retooling the movement; suffice it to say that during the transition period, they examined their mistakes, assessed the existing political situation, commissioned polls to outline appropriate strategy, and then restructured the movement in major ways (Moen 1992). The present characteristics of the Christian Right contrast sharply with previous periods, and explain why the movement is better-positioned today.

One characteristic is a more predictable financial situation. The early organizations banked on direct-mail for their financial support, an unpredictable wellspring because of the ease with which contributors can turn off the flow (Godwin 1988). It is as easy as tossing out repetitious third-class mail. Cognizant of the difficulty of sustaining stable organizations through direct-mail, Christian Right elites emphasized the utility of genuine membership organizations such as Concerned Women for America and Focus on the Family, replete with established dues, meetings, communications, and benefits. They also quietly accepted money from controversial figures such as the Rev. Sun Myung Moon, who helped launch the American Freedom Coalition (Lawton 1988). The latter tactic is more risky, but it keeps the Christian Right flush.

A second characteristic of the Christian Right is a greater representation of theological orientations. Recall that early on the movement consisted mostly of fundamentalists, whose political conservatism and disdain for evangelicals/charismatics was often intense. Pat Robertson's candidacy attracted evangelicals and charismatics into the movement (Hertzke 1993), thereby increasing diversity. While "religious particularism" is a major obstacle to a unified movement (Jelen 1991), it is not necessarily injurious to achieving common goals, since people can operate within the confines of the theological tradition they find most appealing. Moreover, the sectarian attitudes that have haunted the

Christian Right show some signs of abating. Oldfield (1990) found that political activism had a homogenizing and moderating effect on Christian Right supporters, which portends greater cooperation. Then too, the intensity of the current "culture war" necessitates alliances by those holding "orthodox" views (Hunter 1991), even if they are somewhat uneasy with their coalition partners. This logic follows the Islamic aphorism, "the enemy of my enemy is my friend." Even if sectarianism does not abate, the infusion of evangelicals/charismatics may still prove beneficial because it increases the pool of potential recruits.

A third characteristic is the ability to frame issues to maximize support. During the expansionist period, Christian Right leaders constantly invoked moralistic language, spawning organizations like Moral Majority and Christian Voice, issuing "moral report cards" on elected officials, and peddling issues with a strong moral component, such as abortion, school prayer, gay rights, and pornography. Today the Christian Right employs the more familiar and widely accepted language of liberalism, with its focus on rights, equality, and opportunity. Virtually all of its issues have been recast in that rhetoric. School prayer is framed as a "student's right" to pray or as an issue of equal opportunity (for religious expression in the schools); abortion is a civil rights issue involving opportunity for the fetus or the "rights of the unborn"; gay rights is a case of homosexuals seeking "special rights" as citizens; vocal prayer at graduation ceremonies is a case of "free speech" for those holding religious values; the ability of voluntary student religious groups to meet on school grounds is one of "equal access"; the content of school textbooks involves "parental rights" to instill proper values in their children. Christian Right leaders also use the invective language of liberalism as a political tactic, blaming cultural elites for "bigotry" and "discrimination" against traditional values. The ill-fated campaign of Vice President Dan Quayle to chastise the fictional television character Murphy Brown during the 1992 election was designed to rally religious conservatives with the language they had assimilated. Using the rhetoric that Americans are accustomed to hearing both maximizes the appeal of issue positions and circumvents the problems connected to religious discourse in a pluralistic society.

Pat Robertson's "Christian Coalition" seems to undermine this point, with its overt religious title. Yet, Robertson has been a driving force behind the rhetorical reorientation, often framing issues in liberal language and accusing the media of "bigotry" for its portrayal of religious conservatives. The name "Christian Coalition" is easily explained as Robertson's attempt to rebuild his religious constituency, following a foray into presidential politics that meant distancing himself from the Christian Right and resigning his ministerial affiliation.

It is conceivable that the Christian Coalition signals a new twist to Christian Right activism — groups with religious titles secretly advancing candidates and issues amidst secular trappings. Bruce (1988) has noted the interesting dilemma facing Christian Right leaders, who must simultaneously "play to the faithful" and participate in a secular political arena. One way they can lessen their problem is quietly to organize religious conservatives to achieve secular political objectives — hence the "stealth candidates" of the 1992 election season. (Another way is using liberal language to advance moralistic goals.) Other explanations for the stealth candidates, of course, are the need for a surprise attack by an outnumbered force, or a media that simply "rediscovered" the Christian Right following years of neglect. Religious conservatives appeared on radar because journalists looked again at the screen.

A fourth characteristic is a reorientation to the grassroots. Recall that during the expansionist period, the Christian Right focused on lobbying Congress, and exhibited clout by setting the agenda; during the transition period, it lost much of its power on the Hill. Christian Right leaders knew it was necessary to shift to other venues, spawning groups like the American Freedom Coalition, expressly to organize religious conservatives in the grassroots. The Christian Right soon infiltrated the Republican party in select locales, paving the way for Pat Robertson's strong performance in the caucus states during 1988. By 1992, the party platform reflected the Christian Right's influence, and a variety of local initiatives aimed at instigating and inculcating a sense of activism among religious conservatives were underway, such as the anti-gay-rights referenda in Colorado and Oregon. Those activities grew naturally out of a shift to the grassroots. This local activity is likely to spread and intensify in the future, with issues involving public education topping the agenda (Moen 1993), because of the school's key role in socializing citizens.

In summary, the Christian Right has changed substantially over time. A decade ago, it consisted of direct-mail lobbies, led by prominent fundamentalists, who championed a moralistic agenda on Capitol Hill; it now consists of a variety of well-established membership organizations, whose leaders use mainstream language and organize followers in the grassroots. The strident campaign to "put God back in government" has been replaced by a quiet effort to rally sympathetic citizens and win elections. The Christian Right has adjusted itself to the traditional practices of American politics.

CONCLUSION

Evidence and reason suggest that the Christian Right will march down the same path it has followed since 1987. The forces driving the Christian Right's reorientation in the first place still remain, such as an unfriendly political environment in the nation's capital and a climate of popular opinion that disdains moralism. The Christian Right will continue to offer liberal language and to operate at the grassroots, where its prospects are quite good. It has experienced leaders and ample funds, in part because it draws upon the extensive resources of the Rev. Moon, Pat Robertson, and now James Dobson (Shupe 1990; Fineman 1993); it is engaged in an intense cultural war that motivates followers; it operates outside the realm of a Democratic majority in Washington. Its work would proceed quietly, except for the clamor created by its opponents, who realize that in many ways it is better positioned today than in earlier eras.

At the same time, the Christian Right faces major challenges. It lacks a titular leader who can command immediate attention, like Jerry Falwell could in 1981-1982. It lacks a galvanizing issue comparable to the tax-exempt status of religious schools, the one that ignited fundamentalists in the late 1970s. It still suffers from personal rivalries (Jelen 1991), and now is often blamed for the Republican party's poor performance in 1992 (Leege 1993:23). It faces the same dilemma of virtually all other interest groups: retaining its fervent supporters while trying to broaden its base of support. Striking a balance between purity and pragmatism will remain problematic for a movement containing political and theological cross-currents.

The evolution of the Christian Right and the challenges it faces in its current form provide scholars many opportunities in the years ahead. Guth and his colleagues (1988) call for further research into the mobilization of religious belief, the challenge presented to the state by religion, and the role of religion as a source of social cleavage. More narrowly drawn topics that might be added to their list include the importance of political symbols to sustaining the Christian Right, the success of its grassroots activism, and the effectiveness of its coalition building. Recent studies of the movement's political thought (Lienesch 1993) and the saliency of religion in the political process (Kellstedt and Leege 1993) demonstrate that divergent methodological approaches are beneficial in illuminating different research questions. The task facing scholars, whose research agendas are helping to shape public discussion of religious issues (see Woodward 1993), is to bring those divergent approaches to the still untapped areas of inquiry.

REFERENCES

Beatty, K. M. and B. O. Walter. 1988. "Fundamentalists, evangelicals, and politics." *American Politics Quarterly* 16:43-59.

Bledsoe, W. C. 1990. "Post Moral Majority politics." Paper delivered at the annual meeting of the American Political Science Association, San Francisco.

Briggs, K. 1981. "Evangelical leaders hail election and ask continuation of efforts." *New York Times* (Jan. 28):8.

Bromley, D. G. and A. Shupe (eds.). 1984. *New Christian Politics*. Macon, GA: Mercer University Press.

Bruce, S. 1987. "Status and cultural defense." *Sociological Focus* 20:242-46.

_____. 1988. *The Rise and Fall of the New Christian Right*. New York: Oxford University Press.

Brudney, J. L. and G. W. Copeland. 1984. "Evangelicals as a political force." *Social Science Quarterly* 65:1072-79.

_____. 1988. "Ronald Reagan and the religious vote." Paper delivered at the annual meeting of the American Political Science Association, Washington, DC.

Buell, E. H., Jr. and L. Sigelman. 1985. "An army that meets every Sunday?" *Social Science Quarterly* 66:426-34.

"Christian Right." 1980. "Christian right equated with Iran's mullahs." *Washington Star* (Sept. 24):4.

Conover, P. J. 1983. "The mobilization of the new right." *Western Political Quarterly* 36:632-49.

Crawford, A. 1980. *Thunder on the Right*. New York: Pantheon.

D'Antonio, M. 1990. "Fierce in the '80s, Fallen in the '90s." *Los Angeles Times* (Feb. 4):M3.

Diamond, S. 1989. *Spiritual Warfare*. Boston: South End Press.

Dionne, E. J., Jr. 1989. "Taking measure of the impact that Moral Majority has left on the American landscape." *New York Times* (June 15):B10.

Falwell, J. 1980. *Listen America!* Garden City, NY: Doubleday.

Fineman, H. 1993. "God and the grass roots." *Newsweek* (Nov. 8):44.

Godwin, R. K. 1988. *One Billion Dollars of Influence*. Chatham, NJ: Chatham House.

Green, J. C. 1993. "Pat Robertson and the latest crusade." *Social Science Quarterly* 74:157-68.

_____ and J. L. Guth. 1988. "The Christian right in the Republican party." *Journal of Politics* 50:150-65.

Guth, J. L. 1987. "The moralizing minority." *Social Science Quarterly* 68:598-610.

_____ and J. C. Green (eds.). 1991. *The Bible and the Ballot Box*. Boulder, CO: Westview Press.

Guth, J. L., T. G. Jelen, L. A. Kellstedt, C. E. Smidt, and K. D. Wald. 1988. "The politics of religion in America." *American Politics Quarterly* 41:825-38.

Hadden, J. K. and A. Shupe. 1988. *Televangelism*. New York: Holt.

_____, J. Hawdon, and K. Martin. 1987. "Why Jerry Falwell killed the Moral Majority," pp. 101-15 in M. Fishwick and R. B. Browne (eds.), *The God Pumpers*. Bowling Green, OH: Bowling Green State University Popular Press.

Hadden, J. K. and C. E. Swann. 1981. *Prime Time Preachers*. Reading, MA: Addison-Wesley.

Harper, C. L. and K. Liecht. 1984. "Explaining the new religious right," pp. 101-10 in Bromley and Shupe, *q.v.*

Harwood, J. 1985. "Religious right, GOP sometimes spar." *St. Petersburg Times* (Jan. 28):8.

Hastey, S. 1981. "Carter." *Baptist Press* (May 28):1.

Hatch, O. 1983. "Christian conservatives are a major force on U.S. political scene." *Human Events* (Jul. 9):10-12.

Heinz, D. 1983. "The struggle to define America," pp. 133-48 in Liebman and Wuthnow, *q.v.*

Hertzke, A. D. 1988a. "American religion and politics." *Western Political Quarterly* 41:825-38.

_____. 1988b. *Representing God in Washington*. Knoxville: University of Tennessee Press.

_____. 1993. *Echoes of Discontent*. Washington, DC: CQ Press.

Himmelstein, J. L. and J. A. McRae, Jr. 1984. "Social conservatism, new republicanism, and the 1980 election." *Public Opinion Quarterly* 48:592-605.

Hofrenning, D. 1989. "The agenda setting strategies of religious interest groups." Paper delivered at the annual meeting of the American Political Science Association, Atlanta, GA.

Hunter, J. D. 1991. *Culture Wars*. New York: Basic Books.

Hyer, M. 1980. "Outflanking the right." *Washington Post* (Oct. 21):8.

Jelen, T. G. 1987. "The effects of religious separatism on white Protestants in the 1984 presidential election." *Sociological Analysis* 48:30-45.

_____. 1991. *The Political Mobilization of Religious Belief*. New York: Praeger.

Johnson, S. D. and J. B. Tamney. 1982. "The Christian right and the 1980 presidential election." *Journal for the Scientific Study of Religion* 21:123-31.

_____, and R. Burton. 1993. "Family values versus economy evaluation in the 1992 presidential election." Paper delivered at the annual meeting of the American Political Science Association, Washington, DC.

_____. 1989. "Pat Robertson." *Journal for the Scientific Study of Religion* 28:387-99.

Jorstad, E. 1981. *The Politics of Moralism*. Minneapolis: Augsburg.

Kater, J. L., Jr. 1982. *Christians on the Right*. New York: Seabury Press.

Kellstedt, L. A. and D. C. Leege. 1993. *Rediscovering the Religious Factor in American Politics*. Armonk, NY: Sharpe.

Kellstedt, L. A., P. Kellstedt, and C. Smidt. 1990. "Evangelical and mainline Protestants in the 1988 presidential election." Paper delivered at the annual meeting of the American Political Science Association, San Francisco.

Kellstedt, L. A., J. C. Green, J. L. Guth, and C. Smidt. 1993. "Religious voting blocs in the 1992 election." Paper delivered at the annual meeting of the American Political Science Association, Washington, DC.

Langenbach, L. 1988. "Evangelical elites and political action." Paper delivered at the annual meeting of the American Political Science Association, Washington, DC.

Lawton, K. 1988. "Unification church ties haunt new coalition." *Christianity Today* (Feb. 5):46.

Leege, D. C. 1993. "The decomposition of the religious vote." Paper delivered at the annual meeting of the American Political Science Association, Washington, DC.

Liebman, R. C. 1983. "Mobilizing the Moral Majority," pp. 49-73 in Liebman and Wuthnow, q.v.

_____ and R. Wuthnow (eds.). 1983. *The New Christian Right*. New York: Aldine.

Lienesch, M. 1982. "Christian conservatism as a political movement." *Political Science Quarterly* 97:403-25.

_____. 1993. *Redeeming America*. Chapel Hill: University of North Carolina Press.

Linder, R. 1982. "Militarism in Nazi thought and in the American religious right." *Journal of Church and State* 24:263-79.

Lipset, S. M. 1982. "Failures of extremism." *Society* 20 (1):48-58.

Lorentzen, L. 1980. "Evangelical life style concerns expressed in political action." *Sociological Analysis* 41:144-54.

Martz, L., V. E. Smith, D. Pederson, D. Shapiro, M. Miller, and G. Carroll. 1987. "God and money." *Newsweek* (Apr. 6):16-22.

Miller, A. H. and M. P. Wattenberg. 1984. "Politics from the pulpit." *Public Opinion Quarterly* 48:301-17.

Miller, W. E. 1985. "The new Christian right and fundamentalist discontent." *Sociological Focus* 18:325-26.

Moen, M. C. 1988. "Status politics and the political agenda of the Christian right." *Sociological Quarterly* 29:429-37.

_____. 1989. *The Christian Right and Congress*. Tuscaloosa: University of Alabama Press.

_____. 1992. *The Transformation of the Christian Right*. Tuscaloosa: University of Alabama Press.

_____. 1993. "The preacher versus the teacher." *Thought & Action* 9:125-43.

Morin, R. 1993. "Getting a hold on the religious right." *Washington Post Weekly Edition* (Apr. 5-11):37.

Morken, H. 1990. "Religious lobbying at the state level." Paper delivered at the annual meeting of the American Political Science Association, San Francisco.

Nyhan, D. 1980. "Attacks on religious right put its influence in doubt." *Boston Globe* (Oct. 28):1-2.

Oldfield, D. 1990. "The Christian right and state Republican parties." Paper delivered at the annual meeting of the American Political Science Association, San Francisco.

_____. 1992. "The Christian right in the 1992 campaign." Paper delivered at the annual meeting of the Northeastern Political Science Association, Providence, RI.

Ogintz, E. 1980. "Evangelists seek political clout." *Chicago Tribune* (Jan. 13):5.

Ostling, R. N. 1987. "TV's unholy row." *Time* (Apr. 6):60-67.

Pressman, S. 1984. "Religious right." *Congressional Quarterly Weekly Report* 38 (Sept. 12):2315-19.

Shupe, A. 1990. "Sun Myung Moon's American disappointment." *Christian Century* 107:764.

_____ and W. Stacey. 1983. "The Moral Majority constituency," pp. 103-16 in Liebman and Wuthnow, q.v.

Sigelman, L., C. Wilcox, and E. H. Buell, Jr. 1987. "An unchanging minority." *Social Science Quarterly* 68:876-84.

Simpson, J. H. 1983. "Moral issues and status politics," pp. 187-205 in Liebman and Wuthnow, q.v.

Smidt, C. 1983. "Evangelicals versus fundamentalists." Paper delivered at annual meeting of the Midwest Political Science Association, Chicago.

_____. 1987. "Evangelicals and the 1984 election." *American Politics Quarterly* 15:419-44.

_____. 1988. "The mobilization of evangelical voters in 1980." *Southeastern Political Review* 16:3-33.

Spring. B. 1984. "Some Christian leaders want further political activism." *Christianity Today* (Nov. 9):40-41.

Wald, K. D. 1987. *Religion and Politics in the United States*. New York: St. Martins.

_____. 1992. *Religion and Politics in the United States*, 2nd ed. New York: St. Martins.

_____, D. Owen, and S. Hill. 1989a. "Habits of the mind?," pp. 93-108 in T. G. Jelen (ed.), *Religion and Political Behavior in the United States*. New York: Praeger.

_____. 1989b. "Evangelical politics and status issues." *Journal for the Scientific Study of Religion* 28:1-16.

Wilcox, C. 1986. "Evangelicals and fundamentalists in the new Christian right." *Journal for the Scientific Study of Religion* 25:355-63.

_____. 1987. "Popular support for the Moral Majority in 1980." *Social Science Quarterly* 68:157-66.

_____. 1989. "Evangelicals and the Moral Majority." *Journal for the Social Scientific Study of Religion* 28:400-14.

_____. 1992. *God's Warriors*. Baltimore, MD: Johns Hopkins University Press.

Woodward, K. L. 1993. "The rites of Americans." *Newsweek* (Nov. 29):80-82.

Unger, A. 1980. "TV ads try to offset religious right." *Christian Science Monitor* (Oct. 21):6.

Epilogue

On Being "Right" and Religious: A Plea for Complexity

William H. Swatos, Jr.

Editor, Sociology of Religion: A Quarterly Review

> [O]ur ability to have a religious experience depends on whatever metaphor our feeble intelligence can grasp, because our sense of reality isn't that good. (Foster 1985:157)

Through a selection process of which I am unaware, I have been included in the second through fourth editions of *Who's Who in Religion*. When I completed the information form for the last of these, there was an item that asked something like "political affiliation," and I filled in, honestly, Republican. In the questionnaire, this item did not particularly seem to stand out to me; I completed it in much the way I would have, say, "blood type." When the published copy appeared, however, the very last word, standing all by itself immediately before my address, was "Republican."[1] There came to mind the Bible verse, "What I have written, I have written" (John 19:22), though it hardly puts me in good company.[2]

---

[1] Although I am vain, I am not vain enough to buy a copy of *Who's Who* to see myself listed in it; thus while I have seen the print copy of my own biography, I did not see those of others. As I was working on this essay, it occurred to me that there might be some sociological value in seeing how other biographees handled this issue. I conducted a systematic random sample that yielded the following data: Of 87 names, 77 contained appropriate data (the other 10 were either listings where extremely sketchy data were provided by the Marquis company without the collaboration or consent of the biographee, or were biographees from outside the United States; see Who's Who 1994). Of these 77, 14 (18%) indicated Republican preference, 9 Democrat (12%), 54 (70%) no indication. (I don't know what they would have done about blood type!) A cursory examination of the data of those who did state a preference did not indicate any vast difference among them; however, Roman Catholics were dramatically underrepresented proportionally among those stating a preference. No Roman Catholic clergy in the sample indicated a political preference. I do think this volume could be mined in a variety of ways in subsequent research projects; unfortunately, the series does not extend historically far enough to speak definitively to the OCR/NCR distinctions I will discuss in this essay.

[2] All Bible references in this essay are to the New Testament of the Authorized ("King James") Version. The title "Authorized Version" comes from the fact that this translation was authorized for public reading in the Church of England; King James I was Supreme Governor of the Church of England at the time.

But, yes, I am a Republican, and with the exception of Richard Nixon, I have voted consistently for Republican candidates for president and for most other offices. As an Illinois Republican, I particularly enjoyed the time in the 1980s that the LaRouchees managed to get some significant slots as *Democrats* on the November ballot via a lazy primary electorate, but I also was licking considerable wounds after the 1992 election, when Steve Bruce's suggestion that we do this collection first arrived on my desk. This election reminded me that it was a decade before that Republicans in my congressional district defeated themselves during the primary by rejecting a middle-of-the-road, relatively senior incumbent (Tom Railsback) for an ultraconservative who was subsequently bested in November by a man who is now one of the most liberal Democrats in the House (Lane Evans).[3] Something not unlike this also occurred in the 1992 Senate election, when one of the best Republicans on the Democratic side of the aisle in Washington (Alan Dixon) was defeated in the primary, while the Republicans put forward a weak candidate who could not possibly mount a serious challenge to Carol Moseley Brown, the first black woman ever elected to the United States Senate. As someone who also lives on the Iowa border and teaches in that state, I have been able to observe Iowa politics first hand as well. In the 1992 election there I was particularly intrigued to watch how a state-level Equal Rights Amendment was turned from a *women's rights* issue for its proponents, which I am convinced would have passed easily a decade earlier, to a *gay rights* issue by its (largely NCR) opponents, and defeated — this in spite of support for the amendment by virtually all mainline denominations.

I am also a conservative Republican. As a "Young Republican" in college I worked actively for Barry Goldwater, including being involved in a heckling incident of vice-presidential candidate Hubert Humphrey in Lexington, Kentucky, that made network news. In my head as well as my heart I still believe that Goldwater could have brought a resolution to the Viet Nam conflict that would have saved thousands of lives of all the peoples involved in that debacle — even if it did so negatively, by Congress refusing to grant his extreme position rather than being misled by Johnson's prevarication. More recently, I voted for Pat Buchanan in the 1992 primary, not expecting him to win, but to send a conservative message to the Bush campaign. I would have preferred Dan Quayle to either Bush or Buchanan. *Mutatis mutandis technologicus* I am likely today to come out on any issue just to the left or right of Teddy Roosevelt. When some academic friends find this out, they are likely — if they are not totally speechless — to say something like, "So, you're part of the New Christian Right (NCR)." To this I am initially wont to reply, "No, I'm part of the Old Secular Right (OSR)." But that's not quite honest, either, since I am a professing Christian — indeed, I have served as an Episcopalian priest for almost 25 years, though I am hardly comfortable with the political trends of denominational leadership — and, though I never sought it, I have had contact with the *700 Club* through pastoral relationships.

---

[3] The Illinois 17th Congressional District is politically interesting in that while its primary economic base is agricultural (Ronald Reagan's agriculture secretary John Block hails from here), it also is "the Farm Implement Capital of the World," which means a heavy component of union labor.

I suppose, then, one could say I am part of the Old Christian Right. Here's what I mean: As I reflect upon it, for example, George Bush, Gerald Ford, and Barry Goldwater (*inter alia*, Ollie North and Spiro Agnew) are all Episcopalians, as I recall were *both* the Roosevelts. Senator John Danforth (R-MO), Justice Clarence Thomas's principal advocate during his confirmation hearings, though more politically middle-of-the-road than I am, is also an Episcopalian priest, now retiring to devote more time to "Christian service." Eisenhower and Reagan made a stab at being Presbyterians; Quayle did better at it. Gerald Ford attended congressional prayer breakfasts long before they were fashionable, and both he and liberal maverick John Anderson were involved to some degree in the "Christian America" movement of the 1950s. I am old enough to remember both when the phrase "under God" was inserted into the Pledge of Allegiance and when school prayer was banned. I also found it amazing to watch the genuinely evangelical Jimmy Carter defeated by the NCR-backed, eleventh-hour man (see Matt. 20:6), and I can believe that Gerald Ford was sincere in saying that he fixed on his desire to pardon Nixon while in church — indeed, even that Nixon himself was sincere when he asked Kissenger to pray with him.

Maybe it is here, with that almost unimaginable scene of Nixon and Kissenger is supplication before the Almighty, that we begin to hit upon something that is too easily overlooked in attempts to analyze "religion and politics" in the United States: to wit, the complexity of multiple competing variables impacting on real human actors, both as office holders and voters on the one hand, and as people who are or are not in their own eyes "religious" on the other.[4] Jimmy Carter, after all, was not so much defeated by Ronald Reagan as by the economy and the Ayatollah Khomeini. George Bush, similarly, may not have been helped by the Republican platform in 1992, but he was defeated by what Bill Clinton rapidly learned was the real issue: "The economy, stupid." Clinton has had greater success as president, furthermore, precisely in this area, not his left-liberal social agenda. Yet my Bishop, a life-long practicing Democrat, felt he had to vote Republican in 1992, principally over the abortion issue. I have absolutely no doubt in my mind that had George Bush been able to buoy the economy between the end of the Gulf War and November of 1992, he would be president today *with* the 1992 Republican platform as written by the 1992 convention and *not* enacted.

What is the principal difference between the New Christian Right and what I suppose we must call the Old Christian Right? In my view, it is the urgency with which members of the two groups think politics is going to achieve the Kingdom of Heaven on Earth — the extent to which they think human activity can accelerate the Rapture, one of the names of the event that Christians think will occur as the Lord returns and Endtime inbreaks, when we "meet the Lord in the air" (1 Thess. 4:17). The OCR understood politics to be temporal and treated it not too differently from the way Max Weber described it in *Politik als Beruf* (1946 [1919]) — a kind of dirty business that can and should be kept from

---

[4] I have discussed some of these issues, but not with specific reference to the NCR, in earlier essays; see especially Swatos 1990, 1993.

total evil by good men (and, today, women) who see compromise as a virtue in a sinful world rather than as a sin against a putative holy commonwealth. The NCR sees politics as a vehicle for the inbreaking of something far more spectacular. The result is a militancy that was unknown two decades ago.[5]

Indeed, there is something of an irony here, captured by Randall Collins's Furfey Lecture on the shifting uses of "liberal" and "conservative" through time (1993). A hundred years ago, those who sought to integrate religion and politics were known as the Social Gospel movement, and much of their vision, shorn of "Kingdom" rhetoric (for an example of which, written in a specifically sociological context, see Rauschenbusch 1896), was incarnated in the social policies of FDR. Their agenda is basically consistent with that of left-liberals today, and it is still embraced by the liberal Protestant denominations as well as "peace and justice" Catholics. This agenda and some of its original religious tone lie close to the core of the message of the Rev. Jesse Jackson, for example, and because of the connection of the Social Gospel to nineteenth-century millennialism, I am not surprised that there is some overlap discovered between supporters of Jackson and supporters of NCR candidate Robertson (see, e.g., Wilcox 1992). The OCR, by contrast, has generally stood for the separation of church and state, and the separation of the state and the economy.[6] They are "classical" liberals, who are today not grasped fully by prevailing terminological dichotomies. (In my own case, for example, I would vote Libertarian, except that Max Stackhouse long ago convinced me that anyone who took Max Weber's analysis of politics seriously was not acting with ethical responsibility if she or he voted for third-party candidates in the United States.)

Many writers have discussed the millennialism that characterized the United States as the nineteenth century wore on; the dawn of the twentieth century failed to bring the inbreaking of "the Kingdom." One result was secular political

---

[5] The "Fundamentalism Project" notwithstanding (see, e.g., Marty and Appleby 1991), it is religious *militancy*, as Gene Schoenfeld has pointed out (1987), not fundamentalism, that is the new phenomenon since the watershed year of 1979 (see Demerath 1994).

[6] The issue of separation of church and state for the OCR helps me, at least, explain the otherwise anomalous finding of Woodrum and Hoban (1992) that among a relatively conservative religious population there is *greater* support for the teaching of "creationism" in schools than for prayer in schools. I think a certain OCR segment would find legitimacy for the ban on prayer as a valid constitutional separation of religion from the state (consider, e.g., what began as the largely anti-Catholic body, Christians and Others [now Americans] United for Separation of Church and State; or the intriguing relationship between the NRA's concerns about constitutional issues *re* firearms and the Branch Davidian debacle [as detailed by Lewis 1994]), while alternatively interpreting a ban on the teaching of creationism as a challenge to academic freedom. (Note that Woodrum and Hoban's data come from North Carolina, the state where Bruce claims "conscience clause" in education was passed by the legislature in 1979. Note, too, that while support for creationism exceeded support for school prayer in their data by 10 percent, the relative levels were almost three-fourths and two-thirds of the sample, respectively.) In my view the best sociological exposition of the OCR position is to be found in the writings of Peter Berger (e.g., 1970, an essay provoked by the *Left* but, when read carefully, equally applicable to differentiating OCR from NCR world views).

liberalism.[7] This, nevertheless, has left undaunted those whose expectations for the return of Christ have millennialist components.[8] The end of the twentieth century marks another opportunity for the Kingdom. Thus the NCR, like what one might demarcate the OCL (Old Christian Left), has turned to political issues with an *urgency* that is quite different from the OCR's reserve. Though members of the OCR may affirm creedally week by week that "He shall come again with glory," I suspect that most also subconsciously add: "but not any time soon." Ironically, since the NCR socioreligious agenda has had virtually no success, the religious group that has benefitted the most from the NCR are probably Jews, particularly in the state of Israel, who play a special role in many millennialist expectations. (This may be one of the few places where Southern Baptists Clinton and Gore can sit down comfortably at prayer with Jesse Helms.) An Old Christian Right position regarding Israel would be much more pragmatic, while the Christian Left seems to have thrown its sympathies clearly to the Palestinians.[9]

I have been a conservative Republican Episcopalian among conservative Republican Episcopalians. The Diocese of Quincy, where I live, is considered by many the most conservative in the United States. As I write we are in the midst of the national consent-getting process following an episcopal election (for the bishop who will be Quincy VIII); we may well fail. Some locally see this as the beginning of a "constitutional crisis" in the Episcopal Church; I do not. A similar event took place here a century ago with the failed election of James Reginald DeKoven. Historians write of "the DeKoven affair," and some Episcopalians honor him as a saint, but the institutional church rolled along with hardly a jostle. I think that is even more likely to be the case today. The unacceptable error of the present bishop-elect is that he has affirmed the position of a diocese that refuses to recognize the ordination of women to the priest-

---

[7] The transmutation of the Social Gospel movement into secular political liberalism, however, is what makes notions of "secularization" so murky and fraught with traps. (It is for this reason that I think Jeffrey Hadden's discussion of secularization theory [1987] is more on target than Steve Bruce does.) Consider sabbatarianism: Today it would be hard to catch a political liberal breathing notions of Sunday closing. Even the NCR soft-pedals this one. Yet the Christian Left (OCL) used the "day of rest" to advocate *for* laborers who were being worked to death. Was this a "secularizing" of something religious or a casting of a "secular" problem in religious language? Furthermore, though sabbatarianism is largely a thing of the past (Peter Kivisto's visit to Cornwall notwithstanding), the OCL did achieve, with the support of political liberals, the goal of a decent work week, vacations, retirement, and so on. Who succeeded here? Was the OCL bested by secular politicians who took a "practical, businesslike" approach to labor-management relations, or did the OCL inform political decision making — "redeeming the times"?

[8] Premillennialist, *post*millennialist, and *a*millennialist views have each been advanced by Christian theologians with respect to Endtime.

[9] Note that the Israelis virtually declared a holiday upon the election of Bill Clinton. In my view this is because Southern Baptist Clinton was more likely to find their cause tenable than Episcopalian Bush, particularly because Bush's advisers, and more especially Episcopalian Secretary of State Baker, were inclined to OCR compromise, seeing Israel more as a foreign policy issue than a social policy issue. (It should be remembered that Bush switched horses on both the economy and abortion to come onto the Reagan team; Mrs. Bush probably more accurately represents his true feelings and the attitude of the OCR.)

hood (or episcopate) and refuses to consider practicing homosexuals for admission to the ordination preparation process. This candidate assumed the lead on the first ballot and was elected easily on the third. My best estimate, based on both vote tallies and qualitative forays, is that two-thirds of the diocese agree with his position.

The people among whom I live and work support strongly the work ethic, familism, law and order, and something that they would recognize ideal typically as "the American way of life." They are not racists, but they do not support affirmative action. They are not sexists, but they reject feminism. They are not gay bashers, but they oppose gay rights. They are urbanized in the sense that they know what they are "supposed" to think, feel, and say; but they also confide in hushed tones that the truth is otherwise. At the same time, the politics of the NCR repulses them. This politics lacks both refinement and a proper regard for the separation of church and state. It is shrill, while they are quiet. Characteristic of this attitude is the observation of one churchwoman to me: "I'm both pro-choice and anti-abortion; so nobody likes me." *Both/and* is, ironically, the one stance that *both* the "correct" Left *and* the "committed" NCR can anathematize.[10] The bulk of the electorate, however, does not divide so clearly; thus the difficulty of making "sense" — the ultimate sociological endeavor — out of data drawn from election surveys or organizational analyses.[11]

There is much about the NCR that we do not know. We do know that it mobilizes churches, or at least it has done so. Pastors raise a cause, and laity respond. There is nothing new about this pattern. Different denominations on various occasions in United States history have engaged in it. Prohibition and abolition were both "preached" causes, as were civil rights and anti-war activity. It is unfortunate that relatively little data exist to tie together clearly the work of the churches at the level of the laity and these more recent moral endeavors encouraged by the clergy. To the best of my knowledge, there has been no systematic attempt to explore the relationship between Viet Nam era veteran status

---

[10] By contrast, *both/and* is the central fulcrum of a traditional Christian understanding of the Christian's spiritual condition: *both* sinful *and* redeemed.

[11] Because, as I indicated earlier, the issue of gay rights has been debated popularly locally in connection with the Iowa ERA amendment, I want to use it to make a point about the difficulties involved in moving back and forth between survey research and human actors. In his chapter, John Simpson presents two GSS items regarding homosexuality and his scaling of them, and defines *liberal* as including those who think that homosexual relations are "sometimes" or "almost always" wrong and those who would allow a homosexual "to teach in a college or university." My qualitative assessment is that "conservative Christians" with whom I interact could well *both* be classed as "liberals" on these measures *and* vote against the Iowa amendment on the basis of concern over "gay rights." Why? Phillip Hammond and his colleagues have the answer: *family* values. My conservative Christians repeat over and over again that they really don't care what consenting adults do with each other; "that's their business." What they *do* care about is their (grand)children. They do not want homosexuals to have access to school teaching positions or the pulpit or Sunday school while children are forming their own sexual identities. They also do not want *either* heterosexual or homosexual pedophiles in these positions, but because this question is not asked in surveys, they do not have an opportunity to express their opinion. The two, however, are *separate issues*; one involves modeling, the other molestation. (I could offer a similar analysis, on the other hand, of the Hammond *et al.* item on school prayer over the distinction between *requiring* and *allowing* prayer. I hope to elaborate further on these issues of method in a subsequent essay.)

and the NCR. What portion of the membership losses that the liberal Protestant churches have experienced are due to unpopular political stances their leadership adopted in an earlier era and still retain — detailed, for example, in one way in Jeffrey Hadden's *The Gathering Storm in the Churches* (1969) and in another by Robert Wuthnow's *The Restructuring of American Religion* (1988)?

To return to the case of the Diocese of Quincy again, we can see played out the difficulty of choice between duality (both/and) and dichotomy. Quantitatively, two-thirds of the diocese support a candidate for bishop who may well be rejected by a majority of the dioceses of the Episcopal Church in the United States. (If he is *not* rejected, it will almost certainly be because of [1] dioceses *outside* the United States who were the determining bloc in the favorable majority of the last such candidate in the United States [Bishop Iker, Fort Worth]; and [2] intervention in a purely political fashion by interested parties to put pressure on specific dioceses that have voted negatively to change their votes.) Yet, if the failure to gain consents occurs, I cannot foresee more than a third of the diocese voting to begin the process by which it could leave the General Convention of the Episcopal Church.[12] In the specific case of the parish of St. John's, Quincy, which has attempted to withdraw from the Episcopal Church and which is clearly the most conservative congregation in this most conservative diocese, and is now receiving national attention among Episcopalians because it is in litigation against the diocese (the exiting faction having seized the property and assets, valued at over six million dollars), current figures suggest that while about two-thirds of the leadership (vestry) support the withdrawal, two-thirds of the parish do not. (In a congregational vote prior to the withdrawal, the move to withdraw failed to gain a majority; the leadership [some of whom were elected at that same congregational meeting] subsequently voted to take the steps to withdraw.)

What I am trying to demonstrate here is what Tony Blasi describes as the "tentativeness, the casuist nature of much religious conduct" (1990:151), which underlies the broader problem of trying to give analytical fixity to religious meaning. We have in this Diocese of Quincy vignette a clear paradox: a majority of people in a religious group want a leader whose leadership differs from a majority of the leaders of the religious group; yet they want to remain members of the religious group with whose leaders they clearly disagree — *both/and*. I suppose one could say in this case that being "Episcopalian" carries an inner meaning that outweighs external structures of action. One finds the same thing when one visits pastorally in hospitals and discovers that about half the people who put "Episcopalian" in the "religion" blank upon registration have not been in an Episcopal church in twenty years. What's more, when one calls on them, many of these are ready to remonstrate on the errors of the Episcopal Church.

---

[12] The Episcopal Church in the United States is a *confederation* of dioceses; thus, at least in theory, it is possible for a diocese to withdraw from this confederation and remain a part of the Anglican Communion — i.e., "in communion" with the Archbishop of Canterbury. Given the recent action of the Church of England with respect to the ordination of women, however, it is somewhat difficult to understand why this relationship would matter to those opposed to the ordination of women — but, again, if this *is* important, we should take it as evidence for *complexity*, not confusion.

This casuist character of religious life, broadly conceived, seems to be operating at various levels in what we may too easily monochrome in the symbol NCR. For example, a decade ago I did a limited analysis of the local leadership across the United States of a single protest event sponsored by the National Federation of Decency (now the American Family Association; see Swatos 1988). The data have many flaws. Nevertheless, several findings stood out that pertain to the questions I am now raising: A significant majority of these individuals were *not* members of the Moral Majority or regular activists for NCR causes (though among the *small* number of those who were activists, with the exception of one individual who did religious leafleting, all protested against abortion). They did, on the other hand, vote regularly and attend religious activities more than once a week. They were of above average education and income, and white. (This snapshot picture generally corresponds to the more significant, in-depth studies of Warner [1988] and Ammerman [1987].) Most also did *not* think they would participate in a subsequent protest event. This last datum underscores particularly the unpredictability of religious action that is intended in such descriptions of the modern religious condition as *bricolage* or religion *à la carte*.

In closing, I want to tell two more local interest, personal stories to try to illustrate my point about complexity, politics, and religion.

In the fall of 1994, one of my former parishioners declared her candidacy as a Democrat for the Illinois House of Representatives. Until the time that she came soliciting assistance for the primary, for which a voter must declare party affiliation in Illinois, she did not know that both I and her own parents are registered Republicans, and none of us was prepared to change party affiliation. I had not known her all that long, but she and her parents, with whom she is on good terms, go back a ways! In the process we discovered differences of view on many issues (and similarities on a few), about which we might well never have talked otherwise.

In the previous episcopal election (the present bishop, Quincy VII), both I and the rector of the present separating faction of St. John's, Quincy, served on the nominating committee. In the course of our work, I indicated that I would not receive the eucharist at the consecration service if the Presiding Bishop officiated because of my differences from him on what I considered to be essential questions. The rector of St. John's, who is more conservative than I, said he had no problem receiving and seemed to imply that I was a bit silly to have such reservations. Over six months passed between the time of the work on the committee and the service of consecration. During that time, a group of liberal-minded members of St. John's attempted to form a new church in Quincy and were supported in their ultimate success by the then bishop (Quincy VI) and the diocesan Standing Committee. This made the rector of St. John's furious, and he refused to participate in the consecration service of the new bishop (VII). In the meantime, much closer to the service, it became known that other liberal-faction parties opposed to the consecration of Quincy VII were going to refuse to receive the eucharist. A relatively conservative friend who knew my intention phoned me and asked that I please receive in order not to make it appear as though I were supporting this effort. With admitted reservations of conscience, I did so. I attended and received also at the retirement celebration of Quincy VII, in spite of serious personal differences at the time, because he again had in the past few months been attacked with gross unfairness by so-called "liberal" parties principally within the Cathedral congregation.

How do religious motives, religious actions, political motives, and political actions interrelate? Complexly, is the only answer I can give.[13] I think that we probably need to recognize that the New Christian Right *will* inevitably fail, but it will *also* succeed. Both what it does accomplish and does not accomplish of its own agenda will be less than what its opponents fear or it itself hopes, and it will accomplish other things that neither it nor its opponents anticipate, whose effects may or may not coincide with its agenda and may well be more long lasting than those it intended.[14] The combination of material interests and the psychodynamics of human emotions can never be separated from our conduct, ideological considerations not withstanding, and yet to ignore ideology is to ignore how the human mind processes interests and emotions to set out on courses of action that themselves may create new relations of interests, emotions, and ideas.[15]

REFERENCES

Ammerman, N. T. 1987. *Bible Believers*. New Brunswick, NJ: Rutgers University Press.
Berger, P. L. 1970. "Between system and horde," pp. 11-86 in Berger and R. J. Neuhaus, *Movement and Revolution*. Garden City, NY: Doubleday.
Blasi, A. J. 1990. "Problematic of the sociologists and people under study in the sociology of religion." *Ultimate Reality and Meaning* 13: 145-56.
Collins, R. 1993. "Liberals and conservatives, religious and political." *Sociology of Religion* 54: 127-46.
Demerath, N. J. III. 1994. "The moth and the flame." *Sociology of Religion* 55: 105-17.
Foster, G. 1985. *The World Was Flooded with Light*. Pittsburgh, PA: University of Pittsburgh Press.
Hadden, J. K. 1969. *The Gathering Storm in the Churches*. Garden City, NY: Doubleday.
_____. 1987. Toward desacralizing secularization theory. *Social Forces* 65: 587-611.

---

[13] This same theme of complexity regarding conservative Christians was sounded a decade ago by Patrick McNamara in his ASR presidential address (1985) and more recently about religious and political action on a global scale by Jay Demerath in his Furfey Lecture (1994).

[14] In my view this is the point that Bruce *both* makes *and* misses. The NCR will fail *as the* NCR, but once its agenda is out in the political "marketplace," that agenda can take on a life of its own. I do not think FDR thought he was implementing the Social Gospel or that those persons associated with the Social Gospel thought that they were creating New Deal liberalism, but to deny that there are connections is foolish, as I'm sure Bruce would agree. The fact that some of these proposals also were also advanced by "secular" ideologies in no way proves that the OCL had no influence on the historical processes that led to their implementation. With respect to the NCR in particular, we could do worse than study the following observation of Immanuel Wallerstein (1974:59), certainly no friend at this stage of his writing to "culturalogical" arguments: "[I]nitial receptivity of a system to new forms does not lead to gradual continuous change but rather to the stifling of the change, whereas initial resistance often leads later on to a breakthrough."

[15] The last two, admittedly long, sentences constitute, as I see it, the lasting theoretical insight of Weber's Protestant Ethic essays — taken up once again in the address on politics given at the close of his life (see Weber 1930, 1978).

Lewis, J. R. (ed.). 1994. *From the Ashes*. Savage, MD: Rowman & Lifflefield.

Marty, M. E. and R. S. Appleby (eds.). 1991. *Fundamentalisms Observed*. Chicago: University of Chicago Press.

McNamara, P. H. 1985. "Conservative Christian families and their moral world." *Sociological Analysis* 46: 93-99.

Rauschenbusch, W. 1896. "The ideals of social reformers." *American Journal of Sociology* 2: 202-19.

Schoenfeld, E. 1987. "Militant religion," pp. 125-37 in W. H. Swatos, Jr. (ed.), *Religious Sociology*. New York: Greenwood Press.

Swatos, W. H., Jr. 1988. "Picketing satan enfleshed at 7-Eleven." *Review of Religious Research* 30: 73-82.

_____. 1990. "Renewing 'religion' for sociology." *Sociological Focus* 141-53.

_____. 1993. "Back to the future," pp. 185-202 in W. H. Swatos, Jr. (ed.), *A Future for Religion?* Newbury Park, CA: Sage.

Wallerstein, I. 1974. *The Modern World-System*. New York: Academic Press.

Warner, R. S. 1988. *New Wine in Old Wineskins*. Berkeley: University of California Press.

Weber, M. 1930. *The Protestant Ethic and the Spirit of Capitalism*. New York: Scribners.

_____. 1946. "Politics as a vocation," pp. 77-128 in H. H. Gerth and C. W. Mills (eds.), *From Max Weber*. New York: Oxford University Press.

_____. 1978. "Anticritical last word on *The Spirit of Capitalism*." *American Journal of Sociology* 83: 1105-31.

Who's Who. 1994. *Who's Who in Religion*, 4th ed. Wilmette, IL: Marquis Who's Who.

Wilcox, C. 1992. "Religion and the preacher vote in the south." *Sociological Analysis* 53: 323-31.

Woodrum, E. and T. Hoban. 1992. "Support for prayer in school and creationism." *Sociological Analysis* 53: 309-21.

Wuthnow, R. 1988. *The Restructuring of American Religion*. Princeton, NJ: Princeton University Press.

Index